"Nathan Crick's approach to the mechanics of propaganda is a fresh contribution to the conversation and will doubtless be quite useful as students learn how to critically analyze the bewildering propaganda appeals in which we are all immersed."

James J. Kimble, *Seton Hall University, USA*

"'Propaganda' has been a term of abuse for over a century—information we don't like that doesn't seem fair. But as this book demonstrates, propaganda has a distinct meaning, history, and practices related to mass persuasion. In an era of unrelenting mass persuasion, we need this book more than ever."

Ryan Skinnell, *San José State University, USA*

"Nathan Crick's *Propaganda: The Basics* is good to its word: it gets down to the basics of this modern mode of mass communication, and it offers a revaluation of the term on behalf of citizens becoming more critical consumers and more productive creators of public messages. Although keenly aware of the dangers all too present in democracies today, Crick provides both a tool kit and an argument for political speech that can be both ethical and effective."

Robert Hariman, *Northwestern University, USA*

PROPAGANDA

This concise and accessible guide makes clear the ubiquity of propaganda so that readers can understand its function in all layers of society, for both good and for ill, and ultimately use it to make their own voice heard.

Propaganda often appears as a paradoxical art: modern society is awash in propaganda and yet many deny consuming it. Using short, easy to understand examples drawn from politics, culture, and advertising from around the world, this book introduces readers to the basic theory, research, and techniques of propaganda from the American Revolution to the present day. It demystifies propaganda for the purpose of democratizing it, revealing it as a form of mass persuasion that is a necessary part of political culture and essential to promoting social movements, social reforms, political agendas, scientific ideas, and aesthetic tastes. The book emphasizes the creative aspect of propaganda while also stressing the need for critical media literacy and ethical judgment.

Filling a major gap in the literature, this book is an essential read for students of persuasion, rhetoric, communication, journalism, advertising, and public relations. It is also ideal for anyone interested in the fundamental principles and tactical forms of propaganda and those approaching the subject for the first time.

Nathan Crick is a professor in the Department of Communication at Texas A&M University, USA. His recent books include *The Routledge Handbook of Rhetoric and Power* (Routledge, 2024), *Rhetorical Public Speaking*, 4th edition (Routledge, 2022), and *The Rhetoric of Social Movements* (Routledge, 2020).

The Basics Series

The Basics is a highly successful series of accessible guidebooks which provide an overview of the fundamental principles of a subject area in a jargon-free and undaunting format.

Intended for students approaching a subject for the first time, the books both introduce the essentials of a subject and provide an ideal springboard for further study. With over 50 titles spanning subjects from artificial intelligence (AI) to women's studies, *The Basics* are an ideal starting point for students seeking to understand a subject area.

Each text comes with recommendations for further study and gradually introduces the complexities and nuances within a subject.

PROJECTION DESIGN
Davin E. Gaddy

ETHNOGRAPHY
Susan Wardell

BAYESIAN STATISTICS
Thomas J. Faulkenberry

FAT STUDIES
May Friedman

PROPAGANDA
Nathan Crick

For more information about this series, please visit: www.routledge.com/The-Basics/book-series/B

PROPAGANDA

THE BASICS

Nathan Crick

Routledge
Taylor & Francis Group

NEW YORK AND LONDON

Designed cover image: Greg Terranova/Getty Images

First published 2025
by Routledge
605 Third Avenue, New York, NY 10158

and by Routledge
4 Park Square, Milton Park, Abingdon, Oxon, OX14 4RN

Routledge is an imprint of the Taylor & Francis Group, an informa business

© 2025 Nathan Crick

ISBN: 978-1-003-86328-1 (hbk)
ISBN: 978-1-003-86323-6 (pbk)
ISBN: 978-1-003-60723-6 (ebk)

DOI: 10.4324/9781003607236

Typeset in Bembo
by SPi Technologies India Pvt Ltd (Straive)

CONTENTS

WHAT IS PROPAGANDA?

In March, 2012, a 30-minute video called "KONY 2012" appeared online. Seemingly overnight, this one video captured the attention of viewers across the globe. According to media critic Jamie Cohen, much of the success of the video was its timeliness, appearing just after the initial successes of the Arab Spring and Occupy Movements when "people felt the internet may be a force for good" and began to have faith in "digital institutions and social media platforms to usher in a connected world." Created by Jason Russell, founder of the nonprofit Invisible Children, KONY 2012 was designed to highlight the atrocities of Joseph Kony, a Central African warlord responsible for abducting thousands of children to enslave and turn into soldiers, while displacing more than 2.5 million people throughout the region. But what made the video unique was not its subject matter but its method of solving the problem. The stated aim of the video was to "Make Joseph Kony Famous." The logic was simple but revolutionary. The more people knew of the atrocities of Kony, the more they could leverage influence over opinion leaders in society who in turn could influence policy makers who could then direct resources to capturing or killing him. Young people watching the video could then send for an "action kit" that included buttons, posters, stickers, and t-shirts, many of them with Kony's face on them. On April 20, 2012, they were then to "Cover the Night" with posters and messaging so that no one in the world would wake up on April 21 and not know Kony's name. In this

DOI: 10.4324/9781003607236-1

way, every single individual, no matter their age or position, could make a difference. Russell had found a way to mobilize the internet generation for the cause of justice.

Reflecting on his own experience with the video, Cohen recounts the moment when he realized that it was "an exquisite piece of video propaganda." Somewhat embarrassingly, Cohen notes that it was actually the students in his social media class that brought the video to his attention. This was hardly a surprise, for as at the time, KONY 2012 seemed unstoppable. Just as the video had intended, celebrities like Oprah Winfrey, Justin Bieber, Rihanna, and Kim Kardashian all promoted the video, leading to its YouTube viewership increasing from 66,000 to 100 million in just over a week. Acting on impulse and not desiring to be behind a trend, Cohen played KONY 2012 for his class on the spot before viewing it on his own. Sitting in front of his students during the screening, Cohen was surprised when, during the moment when "the music swelled and the camera panned to images of impoverished Ugandan children," he "started to hear sobbing from the students." Then, when it ended, two of his "students seemed profoundly upset that the merchandise boxes Jason Russell told them to buy were sold out." At that point, Cohen realized that he had just been the medium by which Russell's propaganda could persuade his own students, who ironically had taken the class to learn how to criticize propaganda. Without thinking about it or even realizing it, he had heard, understood, and acted upon the intended message of the video. Cohen summarizes its message this way: "You need to watch this experiment. You will understand YouTube changes the world. You will share this video. You can save Ugandan children," but "only if you *act now, email a celebrity* **and** *buy a kit* before they're sold out." His students heard this message loud and clear, and they felt guilty when they could not follow through.[1] Cohen had become an unwitting propagandist.

Despite the viral success of KONY 2012, its legacy has been far more problematic. First, the ultimate goal of the video was never accomplished. Interest in the video dropped as quickly as it had risen. "Cover the Night" was deemed a failure and Kony remained at large for ten years before reportedly dying of COVID-19 in 2021. Second, its persuasive tactics were called into question. As noted in a 2022 retrospective article by *New York Times* reporter Emma Madden, "People online debated the film's racial politics, the ethics of humanitarianism and the utility of 'slacktivism,' the equation of likes and shares with action." But despite these criticisms, the creator of the video remained proud of what he tried to accomplish. Talking to Madden in a phone interview for the article, Russell said: "The top criticism that I have read about over the years is the oversimplification of a complex issue…To that I would say, 'I hear you, but to make something go viral'—our goal was to simplify a complex issue—'that's what you have to do.' In a sense it's meant as a criticism, but I saw it as a compliment."[2] For Madden, however, the importance of the video was its prophetic function: "At a time when a constant stream of videos on TikTok, Instagram and Twitter is illustrating the real-time destruction of Ukrainian cities by Russian forces, the film reads as both a relic of what experts have described as a techno-optimistic post-Arab Spring digital landscape and a precursor to an era of seemingly endless footage of violence and conflict on social media." KONY 2012 had hoped that by highlighting violence it could put an end to violence. But instead the video highlighted the fact that social media could never get enough of violence.

I introduce a book on propaganda with the case of KONY 2012, first and foremost, to move past popular stereotypes that work to blind us to the workings of propaganda in modern society. Too often, the word "propaganda" calls to mind the representative tactics of 20th-century totalitarian regimes that were so masterfully captured and caricatured by George Orwell's *Nineteen Eighty-Four,* such as the incendiary speech, the orchestrated rally, the rigid uniform, the iconic flag, the graphic poster, the storm trooper, and the partisan press. In popular usage, propaganda represents less a set of persuasive tools than it does a medium for lies, coercion, hate, and mass manipulation. To label something as "propaganda" is to claim that a message is not what it purports to be, but is in fact a cover for hidden interests that uses disinformation and emotional appeals to seduce and exploit its audience.

But there is a problem with this approach. If we were to use this definition, can we accurately label KONY 2012 as propaganda? To be sure, one can justifiably argue that the video presented an "oversimplification of a complex issue" and used framing devices that appealed to racial stereotypes, among other issues. But there was nothing particularly deceptive about the production. Russell claimed it as his own campaign, presented a set of relatively accurate facts, was open about his aims and methods, and used the profits and resources to genuinely try to capture Joseph Kony and help children escape a life of slavery and violence. If this is *not* propaganda, then the term's meaning must be restricted only to cases of egregious disinformation and hate speech. But if it *is* propaganda, then we must come to terms with the larger implication that in the digital age, all of us consume and often produce propaganda on a daily basis, sometimes unwittingly but more often deliberately and eagerly.

This book is based on the second premise that propaganda is best viewed as a set of modern techniques for producing mass persuasion that has become ubiquitous in our digital media environment. This approach returns propaganda to the original meaning of the term, which was to designate the aims and methods of the *Congregatio de Propaganda Fide* (Congregation for Propagation of the Faith), an organization of Roman Catholic cardinals founded in 1622 to carry out missionary work. Propaganda simply meant, in this early usage, to engage in "propagation," which is defined as the act of widely spreading and promoting something. In the case of KONY 2012, for instance, Madden's article cites Jonah Berger, a marketing professor at the Wharton School of the University of Pennsylvania, who attributed the video's success to the mastery of the STEPPS method: "social currency, triggers, emotion, public practical value and story," which are all factors that "appeal to our psychological makeup and basic human motivations." Berger's approach to this video reflects the approach to propaganda in this book, which is primarily to explore the *how* and *why* of persuasion. The study of disinformation, exploitation, and authoritarianism is undoubtedly a crucial component of propaganda studies. But it is not its only or essential component. Propaganda is primarily a technique of *persuasion*. That lies, hate speech, and covert psyops exist is undeniable and a rising threat to democratic life. But from a persuasive perspective, the issue that concerns this book is not *that* they exist, but *how* they are made appealing and *why* audiences consume these messages. After all, people often still believe lies even after they are revealed to be lies. They do so because they find the lies more attractive than the truth. Until we understand the basic propaganda tactics and persuasive appeals, we will neither be able to resist nor improve propaganda.

As a long-time teacher of propaganda, I also have another, more explicitly rhetorical motive in writing this book. I wish to make citizens better propagandists in their own right. Having taught hundreds of students over two decades, I have never encountered a single young person who was not enthusiastic to learn these techniques and use them to advance their own causes. They all see the dangers of propaganda in the wrong hands. They all perceive the threat of media concentration, consolidation of power, hyper-partisanship, intolerance, the proliferation of trolls and bots, the spread of fake news, and the weaponization of almost every aspect of social life. But they also wish to be more successful recruiters, activists, salespeople, marketers, organizers, and volunteers. They perceive both the danger of propaganda when it is misused and the necessity of creating better propaganda. They all share the youthful idealism that propaganda campaigns that can expose abuses, highlight possibilities, invite cooperation, and direct action have the potential to be instruments of progress. And most importantly, they all recognize that in a message-dense, interconnected digital environment that crosses national borders, one of the primary means of expressing social, economic, and political power is through propaganda. I believe that democratic society benefits when more people, not less, master the arts of persuasion and use it as a vehicle for exerting influence in their world. I hope that this book can help democratize the art of propaganda and help facilitate the open competition of viewpoints between engaged citizens. After all, those in power hardly need a primer on the techniques of propaganda. They have mastered it already and have ready access to the technologies of production and means of distribution. This book is written for the rest of us who must do more with less, both as critics and as producers.

That said, there is no doubt that embracing these techniques brings considerable ethical challenges and forces sometimes unwanted compromises. Whereas rhetoric, classically understood, focused on orations by single individuals, propaganda often uses anonymous messaging disseminated through the mass media in ways that engulf rather than address an audience. Moreover, sophisticated techniques of data gathering, demographic analysis, covert dissemination, graphic manipulation, and psychological manipulation make propaganda often appear more like an industrial product than an individual art. But the fact remains that in our modern technological society, whether one chooses to produce, criticize, or simply understand the nature of propaganda, propaganda is thrust upon us. There is no escape from its influence. Even those who refuse to consume any media whatsoever, and live in a proverbial cabin in the woods, will have their lives impacted by propaganda because of its influence on legal policies, social norms, economic opportunities, or linguistic conventions. But for everyone else with a smartphone, propaganda not only comes to us directly on our social media feeds but even asks us for our propaganda preferences. One of the purposes of this book is to understand that much of what we willingly consume *is* propaganda, and what makes it propaganda is not necessarily the fact that it is exploitative and full of disinformation (although it very well might be) but because it makes use of a repertoire of persuasive techniques adapted to a mass audience. Accepting that we are *already* implicated in the propaganda of our times therefore makes it imperative to become self-aware of what we are consuming, creating, and sharing. Only when we accept propaganda as part of our lives can we begin to actively criticize and resist manipulation, push back against the tide of disinformation, and master the arts of persuasion on our own to make society more democratic and more just.

DEFINING PROPAGANDA

One of the challenges in defining propaganda is that definitions of propaganda are themselves instruments of propaganda. There exists, in other words, a long-established established genre of **antipropaganda propaganda** that defines propaganda in the most derogatory terms (as outright manipulations and lies) in order to attack opponents (by labeling their messages as "mere propaganda") and to flatter one's audience (by telling them that they are too smart to fall for such nonsense). This definition of propaganda popularized by this genre has become so influential that it is almost common sense. When people use the term "propaganda" they mean the most superficial, false, and manipulative set of lies imaginable that no self-respecting person would produce or consume. This definition of propaganda has long been deemed inaccurate, but altering common sense is not easy. Besides, the epithet "propaganda" is too useful a tool of condemnation to give up lightly. Nonetheless, it is crucial to our collective well-being to broaden the definition of propaganda to include our own preferences and practices; otherwise genuine self-awareness will be impossible. Ironically, the binary logic of anti-propaganda propaganda actually makes us more susceptible to propaganda's influence by making it only something "other" people consume. It tells us that if we believe a message to be sincere, right, and true, then it cannot be propaganda. But once we remove a whole class of messages into the "safe" category, we lose the ability to critically analyze them. And that is why anti-propaganda propaganda is so effective at spreading propaganda under a different name.

The definition I give of propaganda seeks to capture all of its universal qualities while leaving out anything contingent or variable. This definition therefore excludes many of the characteristics often assumed to be "essential" parts of propaganda, including such things as its reliance on lies, its covert character, its exploitation of division, and its use as an instrument of domination. Undoubtedly, much propaganda might accurately be described in this way, but that does not make these *essential* qualities. Rather, these characteristics mark it as a kind of propaganda known as **disinformation**, which is the deliberate spreading of falsehoods with the intention to deceive. But successful propaganda may also be factual, open, unifying, and even liberating, as one might think of the propaganda of the Civil Rights Movement. It is important not to equate propaganda with disinformation if we are to understand the full range of its techniques. However, at the same time that a definition of propaganda must leave contingencies out, it must also *include* essential qualities that make it distinct from communication, persuasion, and rhetoric. By means of contrast, **communication** is the symbolic sharing of meanings, **persuasion** is the use of symbols to change attitudes and beliefs, and **rhetoric** is the art of persuasion that seeks to direct action and constitute judgment within a situation marked by uncertainty and urgency. Propaganda may include all of these characteristics but adds characteristics that warrant a category of its own. The definition that I believe best captures its essential qualities is this: **propaganda** *is a set of modern techniques for producing, organizing, and directing the reflexes of a mass of individuals by creating events, crafting identity, simplifying ideas, and arousing passions.* By focusing exclusively on its characteristic means of persuasion, this definition invites us to see propaganda as a ubiquitous practice that is inescapable in our digital age. Let us break down this definition into its component parts:

Propaganda Is a Set of Modern Techniques

Propaganda is a *modern* phenomenon, which means that it arose in the postindustrial era that saw the rise of modern statistical and empirical sciences. Unlike the art of rhetoric in the Greek world, which was based largely on personal experience of trial and error, modern **techniques** are grounded in social scientific methods that have largely been stripped of their cultural specificity or personal flair and have been turned into mathematical formulas that guarantee universal outcomes. To observe modern techniques at work, simply observe the ways that algorithmic logics have made objects from cars to smartphones to restaurants to social media apps all converge to an almost identical form of an interface regardless of its place of origin. Modern techniques provide formulas for success that are often felt to be necessary if one is to survive in a competitive field. The prevalence of such techniques was brought to public attention in spectacular fashion in 2018 after a whistleblower at a propaganda firm called Cambridge Analytica revealed how it used surreptitiously obtained data from millions of Facebook users to help construct 253 personality profile types that could be plugged into algorithms to help place highly personalized ads and content (including political content) on their social media feeds without their knowledge. The revelation contributed to the company's dissolution, but in reality Cambridge Analytica was simply exploiting the best available modern techniques at hand to produce data-driven behavior change.[3]

For Producing, Organizing, and Directing the Reflexes

The goal of propaganda is not to change minds or inculcate belief for its own sake; it is to produce action. If changing ideas is necessary to produce action, then propaganda will pursue persuasion in that way as a means to an end, but only insofar as it brings about a tangible outcome. The goal is to generate a reflex, which is a habitual response to recurrent stimuli that is grounded in a feeling of valuation and which can be recognized by others as indicating that one belongs to a group. Propaganda therefore sets for itself the task of producing these reflexes by presenting models for stimulus response, then providing a group identity to which those reflexes are bound, and finally directing these reflexes toward variable ends that are felt to be timely, effective, and justified. Brand loyalty, team spirit, political partisanship, fan culture, and patriotic nationalism are all examples of these types of organized reflexes. In 1994, for instance, the nation of South Africa changed its flag after the fall of apartheid, replacing the previous flag that had been used since 1928. The new state under Nelson Mandela had to work to shift the patriotic reflex from one symbol to another, investing the new flag with an inclusive meaning capable of uniting previously separate groups under a single banner, particularly on the sports field.[4]

Of a Mass of Individuals

The consumers of propaganda are also characteristically **mass individuals** whose lives and livelihoods are dependent on the institutions and resources of a postindustrial technological society. Propaganda understood in this way only arose in the late 19th century with the rise of the nation state, global economies, and the mass media, urban concentration, the spread of literacy, and rapid industrialization. Previous to this time, the vast majority of people remained illiterate and bound to a local, agricultural economy. Complex, argumentative debate was largely confined to a literary elite while the vast majority of people were subject only to the most basic symbolic appeals of loyalty and allegiance. Today, in contradistinction, vast numbers of people who live in an industrial society are educated, mobile, specialized, diverse, and eager consumers of media and messages. They are individuals because they are no longer bound by the conservative, traditional norms of self-contained communities. Instead these individuals each see themselves as unique. But they are members of a mass because, despite their uniqueness, they are all exposed to the same messages and must navigate the same technological society. Hence we have the phenomenon of social media apps inviting the user to individualize their preferences by selecting from same variety options that are offered to millions of other users. Similarly, in 2023 the streaming music service Spotify introduced a new artificial intelligence DJ, called "X," that would curate tailor-made playlists using a human-sounding DJ speaking directly to the user on a first-name basis. This individualization, however, was matched by the mass effect of every single Spotify user having the exact same DJ who used the same repertoire of stock phrases and manner of address, thereby treating everyone exactly the same.[5]

By Creating Events

Propaganda is not just about creating and disseminating messages. It is about manufacturing events that themselves become the subject and source of messages. An **event** is a sequence of happenings and changes in continuous time that can be characterized as having a single, dominant quality. The propagandist actively engages with the material of lived reality to construct events that engage attention and interest while promoting specific attitudes or arousing specific responses. These include the genres of the publicity stunt, a fundraiser, the press conference, the convention, the grand opening, the lobbying effort, the policy proposal, the research agency, or the covert operation. Some of these events are overtly persuasive, like the campaign rally, while others are covert, like a counterintelligence operation. Either way, propaganda does not just have to wait for events to happen before responding. Propagandists can often write the response first and then manufacture the event to conform to the script. In this way, propaganda guarantees that its message will be timely because it responds immediately to the event that the propagandist has deliberately produced. During the 2024 Summer Olympics, for example, Paris Mayor Anne Hidalgo swam in the River Seine in advance of the outdoor swimming events that would be held in the river. This event attracted widespread media attention and was used to showcase the improvement in the river's waters and the overall ecological state of the once-polluted waterway.[6]

Crafting Identity

Although propaganda still makes use of classical strategies of ethos that seek to increase the credibility of the speaker, propaganda expands the concept of those to include the constitution of the identity of the consumer of propaganda as well. One can still find traditional ethos expressed in the political speech, the endorsement, the spokesperson, the sponsorship, or the charitable donation. But very often, propaganda has no clear "speaker" at all. The message comes, as it were, from no one in particular, as one might think of graffiti on a wall without a tag. Slogans, rumors, flags, icons, colors, memes, and photographs are just some of the media that we consume that have no clear authorship. Instead, these forms of propaganda seek to create a recognizable **identity**, which is simply a sense of one's character that is attractive to an audience and can be used to establish collective identities in the form of clubs, advocacy groups, voting blocks, fan cultures, unions, gangs, team spirit, or brand loyalty. By creating identities, propaganda establishes a motive of action based less on the identity of the speaker than on the identity of the audience. One of the most famous instances of crafting a collective identity occurred during the lead-up to the 2011 Egyptian Revolution. Later dubbed the "Facebook Revolution," it was catalyzed by the public beating to death of an Egyptian man named Khaled Said, who was assaulted by police for having documented police corruption on a video. A few days after his death, Google executive Wael Ghonim launched the "We Are All Khaled Said" Facebook page, which attracted hundreds of thousands of members and became a space for popular dissent because it established, for the first time, a common revolutionary identity by turning Said into a symbol of life under state oppression.[7]

Simplifying Ideas

Propaganda makes use of every psychological and sociological principle to reduce even the most complex idea to its simplest, most stimulating form. By **idea** I mean any condition of any kind that can be captured in a phrase, from "war is hell" to "red wine reduces heart disease" to "democracy promotes freedom" to "global warming is real." The essence of propaganda, as a form of communication, is its ability to translate even the most pressing, complex, and important topic into a crystallized form that presents stark alternatives, easy answers, catchy slogans, and predictable outcomes. Propaganda, to be successful, must always short-circuit reflective thought and sustained inquiry, replacing it with reflex responses, snap judgments, and stereotyped impressions. Today, the most perfect expression of simplified propaganda is the meme, which literally reduces any topic to a familiar iconic representation paired with a witty turn of phrase. But the meme is in many ways just an extension of the long tradition of propaganda posters that pair simplified images with slogans. The People's Republic of China, for instance, has long made use of propaganda posters, notably in enforcing its one-child policy to control population, which often included threatening phrases. But because this policy resulted in population stagnation and a long-term gender imbalance, as parents desired to raise a boy over a girl, recent efforts have been made to overturn this policy by using slogans like: "Caring for the girl means caring for the future of the nation." This phrase encapsulates a widespread national problem and provides a simple solution.[8]

And Arousing Passions

Because propaganda targets a mass audience and is interested less in thought than in reflex, emotional appeals and propaganda play an outstanding role. By **passions** I mean that particular set of emotions that tend to be the most instinctive and volatile. The four passions included here are desire, fear, guilt, and anger. Although propaganda makes use of the entire emotional spectrum, I focus on these four because they are the primary movers of action. Desire is that passion position that propels us forward to attain our goals, while fear is that passion to avoid the pain, suffering, and ruin that would put an end to our desires. Guilt exploits that feeling that we have not lived up to our highest ideals and must somehow redeem ourselves, whereas anger focuses our aggression on what we feel to be the cause of some kind of violation or suffering. Propaganda seeks to arouse these passions by vivid presentations of situations, real or imagined, that are designed to provoke an immediate response. In the days leading up to the Brexit referendum in the United Kingdom, for instance, an advertisement appeared that appealed directly to raw emotions. The ad showed a documentary image of lines of Syrian refugees with the words: "BREAKING POINT. The EU has failed us all. We must break free of the EU and take back control of our borders." The ad thus played on fears of largely non-white immigrants while also channeling anger at the European Union for allegedly forcing the UK to allow them entry.[9]

WHY WE ARE STUCK WITH PROPAGANDA

Our modern world is a product of propaganda, for good or ill. The flood of propaganda messages seeking our attention produces all of the modern neuroses of the modern age—loneliness, distraction, polarization, addiction, stereotyping, groupthink, conspiracy theory, and license. These are particularly pronounced when individuals are isolated from intimate social settings and when they rely upon, or only have access to, single source messaging. But propaganda also enables people access to a vast amount of different perspectives from across the globe. Propaganda functions to stimulate interest, even if only momentarily, in subject matters that would have been unheard of only decades previously. And with digital technologies, average users now have at their disposal the tools to become their own propagandists, whether it be as online influencers or as advocates for some cause. Much of the propaganda that gets produced and disseminated is not pretty. It is created by troll farms, designed by corporate and state interests, fabricated from artificial intelligence, and disseminated by bots. But much of it is also created by living, human beings, many of them belonging to the members of the rising generations eager to participate in and to master the techniques of mass persuasion in order to produce a better future. The fact that authoritarian states are today the ones who most loudly complain about propaganda and seek to restrict the free play of persuasion should tell us something.

Propaganda is here to stay because it is what results when the innate capacity for human beings to persuade one another combines with the technologies and techniques of the modern age. We cannot rid ourselves of propaganda because it is a natural outgrowth of the desire to exert symbolic influence on the widest scale. But we can improve propaganda if we take it seriously as an art. This requires not only training more and better propagandists, but also giving public audiences the tools to be more astute critics of the propaganda that they choose to consume. In sum, the only way to improve propaganda is to teach people to master it, to use it, to criticize it, and to learn from it. I am a democratic humanist to the degree that I believe everyone should be given the freedom and capacity to cultivate their individual powers toward some ideal of the good. Tragically, the propaganda of disinformation exploits this desire for growth by creating polarizing narratives of victimhood and blame that are communicated under false pretenses to serve the interests of the few. Such disinformation and manipulation must be constantly exposed if we are to have any hope for our collective future. But this critical project must also be paired with a productive one. We must recognize that propaganda can also provide individuals with the means to constitute power through symbolic action. To label these practices under a different name in order to cloak it with an aura of virtue and to avoid the taint of "propaganda" is not to engage in analysis but in deflection. All mass persuasion is propaganda because it must necessarily employ the same techniques to appeal to a mass audience. Propaganda is never without its flaws, even under the best of circumstances. But through collective, concentrated, open-minded inquiry, propaganda can and must be turned, as much as is possible, toward the benefit of our common world.

DISCUSSION QUESTIONS

1. What distinguishes propaganda from other forms of communication, like news, argumentation, science, religion, or advertising? What qualities overlap and where do they diverge? And how do you know propaganda when you see it?
2. What type of propaganda do you consume on a regular basis? Why do you choose that form of propaganda and what satisfaction does it provide you? What changes about these consumption habits the moment you label them "propaganda"?

EXERCISES

1. Treat the definition of propaganda as a method of production. Even though you have not yet studied any of the particular methods of persuasion, try your best to invent a campaign that persuades some local audience to adopt a new practice. Make sure to adopt a tactic for every part of the definition.
2. Find the most popular commercials that featured in a past Super Bowl. Identify the aspects of that commercial that forms to the parts of the definition, and specify which tactic was the most important.

SUGGESTED READINGS

The most comprehensive introduction to the history, theory, and practice of propaganda is *Propaganda & Persuasion*, 8th Edition, by

Nancy Snow, Garth S. Jowett, and Victoria O'Donnell. This book uses in-depth case studies to exemplify the workings of propaganda techniques. Particularly when paired with their companion text, *Readings in Propaganda and Persuasion: New and Classic Essays*, it is rightly seen as one of the best broad treatments of the topic.

For sheer historical sweep, the standard history of propaganda is Philip M. Taylor's *Munitions of the Mind: A History of Propaganda*, 3rd Edition. By leaving aside much of the theoretical discussion of propaganda, Taylor provides a highly readable narrative that begins in the Classical World and brings readers up to the Terror Attacks of 9/11.

Lukasz Olejnik's book *Propaganda: From Disinformation and Influence to Operations and Information Warfare* delves into the covert aspects of propaganda that exploit technological capability to target and reach mass audiences undetected.

NOTES

1 Jamie Cohen, "How KONY 2012 trained the audience—and YouTube— to love reactionary media," Medium, March 4, 2002, https://onezero. medium.com/how-kony-2012-trained-the-audience-and-youtube-to- love-reactionary-media-f3c38435ba58.

2 Emma Madden, "'Kony 2012,' 10 years later," *The New York Times*, March 8, 2022, https://www.nytimes.com/2022/03/08/style/kony-2012-invisible- children.html.

3 Alex Hern, "Cambridge Analytica: how did it turn clicks into votes?" *The Guardian*, May 6, 2018, https://www.theguardian.com/news/2018/ may/06/cambridge-analytica-how-turn-clicks-into-votes-christopher- wylie.

4 Craig Ray, "SA's flag symbolises success and unity on the sports fields and doesn't deserve 'burning'," *Daily Maverick*, May 7, 2024, https://www. dailymaverick.co.za/article/2024-05-07-sas-flag-symbolises-success-and- unity-on-the-sports-fields-and-doesnt-deserve-burning/.

5 Benjamin Fredell, "My affair with Spotify's AI DJ," *The Tacoma Ledger*, February 19, 2024.
   https://thetacomaledger.com/2024/02/19/my-affair-with-spotifys-ai-dj/.

6 "Paris Mayor Anne Hidalgo swims in the Seine nine days before Olympic Games kickoff," *France24*, July 17, 2024, https://www.france24.com/en/ france/20240717-paris-mayor-anne-hidalgo-swims-in-the-seine-nine- days-before-olympic-games-kickoff.

7 "Khaled Said: The face that launched a revolution," Abram Online, June 6, 2012, https://english.ahram.org.eg/NewsContent/1/0/43995/Egypt/0/Khaled-Said-The-face-that-launched-a-revolution.aspx.

8 Viv Marsh, "China to overhaul 'threatening' one-child slogans," BBC News, February 27, 2012, https://www.bbc.com/news/world-asia-17181951.

9 Josh Lowe, "Brexit: UKIP launches 'breaking point' immigration poster," *Newsweek*, June 16, 2016, https://www.newsweek.com/brexit-eu-immigration-ukip-poster-breaking-point-471081.

THE FORMATION OF MOTIVE

In the 1960s, backyards across the United States became do-it-yourself construction sites for concrete bunkers. Homeowners who might have enjoyed the grass and trees now thought it necessary to clear a space on which to lay cinder blocks and build an ugly, uncomfortable, rectangular building that they would very likely never use. What motivated this seemingly irrational behavior? The answer can be found in the 1959 pamphlet by the US Office of Civil and Defense Mobilization titled "The Family Fallout Shelter." Distributed widely to the public in print and through public service announcements, this pamphlet urged ordinary citizens to prepare themselves for a possible nuclear attack by the "enemy" (that is, the Soviet Union) by creating a space in which they could find safety. These shelters would be supplied with beds, food, a Geiger counter, an air circulator, and a radio, and they would ideally allow people a place to live for two weeks in the event of a bombing. The pamphlet lays out the need for such a shelter in stark terms:

> Let us take a hard look at the facts. In an atomic war, blast, heat, and initial radiation could kill millions close to ground zero of nuclear bursts. Many *more* millions—everybody else—could be threatened by radioactive fallout. But most of these could be saved. The purpose of this booklet is to show how to escape death from fallout.[1]

Given such "facts," no wonder that many homeowners decided to dig up their gardens and ruin their back patios by building concrete

DOI: 10.4324/9781003607236-2

bunkers. They were driven by a desire to save themselves and their families from the effect of nuclear fallout.

Like all effective propaganda, the pamphlet gave citizens a **motive**, which is a compelling and self-conscious reason for acting. A motive identifies an action and then gives a "why" that specifies qualities of the action, the character of the objects of concern, the desired or feared outcomes, the explanation of cause and effect, and the state of one's emotions. To give an account of our motives, therefore, is to give order and coherence to our actions, no matter how incomprehensible or absurd they might seem to outside observers. Needless to say, the actual cause of our behavior is always more complicated, messy, and mysterious than our reflexive accounts of why we do what we do. Much of our action occurs, in fact, without any deliberate thought at all—and for good reason. If we had to think about and have a reason for everything we did during the day, our minds and bodies would be exhausted and our efficiency would plummet. Nonetheless, when asked to account of ourselves, we will always find a way of explaining a motive that makes sense to ourselves and to others. This does not mean we always want a "good" answer. We simply need to explain our actions in a way that supplies a reason. This process whereby we provide a satisfying account of our behavior we call rationalization. Whereas **reason** is a capacity to use logic, investigate a problem, and arrive at a solution or explanation, **rationalization** is the process of reflecting on past actions and coming up with an account that justifies or at least explains them.

Propaganda, always eager to give its audience what it wants, supplies both reasons and rationalizations to help people both to form and to understand their motivations. To understand how this happens, it is useful to look at motives in a slightly different way than to which we are accustomed. Often, we think of motives as referring to something *inside* the individual's consciousness, as if we can only understand motives by delving deep into the psyche. I suggest it is better to think of motives as shorthand descriptions of external situations—that is, to things *outside* the individuals' consciousness—that make their action seem reasonable. This happens all the time in our daily interactions. Rather than explaining personal aims, or desires, for example, people often respond to the question "why did you do that?" by indicating aspects of the situation as they understood it. A great deal of propaganda therefore works to form our motives not by telling us what to do but rather by defining situations in a way that encourages the action preferred by the propagandist.

Consider a few examples. During the early weeks of the COVID-19 pandemic, stores across the globe were sold out of toilet paper within days after reports that crucial supply chains might be disrupted. In Hong Kong, toilet paper became such a valued commodity that an armed gang robbed a shop of 600 rolls of toilet paper in one day.[2] In the summer of 2024, groups of residents from Barcelona, Spain, began roaming the popular streets and squirting tourists with water pistols. Convinced that mass tourism was destroying the social fabric of the city, they believed their actions would result in limits on the crush of tourists during the summer months.[3] In 2010, in the Canadian province of Saskatchewan, eleven men and one woman posed for photographs while standing partially nude beside a pothole-ridden stretch of highway. Their proximate aim was to create a calendar. When asked for their larger motive, they pointed to the way that government officials had long neglected the road so that it had fallen into extreme disrepair. The calendar not only raised $40,000 but led to the repaving of the road.[4] In all three of these cases, the explanation for their apparently unusual or extreme behavior is found in the way that the actors comprehended the nature of their situation—the breakdown in supply chains, a glut of tourists, or the state neglect of roads. By properly contextualizing their acts, their motives become not only clear but potentially rational.

Propaganda thus seems to have a fairly straightforward task of getting people to accept the definition of a situation and then provide reasons and rationalizations for an appropriate action. But actually getting people to perform that action is never so simple. Indeed, active propagandists who are passionate about their goals and wish to spread their message constantly find it frustrating how slow people are to change. There are many reasons for this fact: 1) We live in a message-dense environment so that even appealing messages are quickly crowded out by others and lost in the flux and chaos of voices. 2) People have limited time and energy, so they conserve as much as they can and therefore tend to process information quickly and often superficially when they have the opportunity. 3) Action is laborious, meaning that actually exerting effort to do something out of one's ordinary routine requires an act of will. 4) Many people simply lack the time, money, education, or opportunity to act even if they wanted to do so. 5) Habit is pleasurable and stubborn, so that if an action requires us to break out routines and move outside our habits, this can be not only disruptive but frightening. In sum, everyone wishes for a better life and a better world. But we also wish to keep what we have and not spend more than we need.

The rest of this chapter will explore some of the psychological foundations of propaganda that are useful in breaking inertia and encouraging people to adopt new behaviors. The goal of propaganda is not only to define motives, but also to generate enough desire in the audience to act on them. The people who built bomb shelters might have felt embarrassed after a decade had passed without incident, but their motive can be easily explained by simply pointing to what was written in the pamphlet: "Your Federal Government has a shelter policy based on the knowledge that most of those beyond the range of blast and heat will survive if they have adequate protection from fallout." The pamphlet described the potential dangers of the situation that would affect all US citizens no matter where they lived. Any rational person, accepting this fact, would thus have constructed a shelter. The nature of the situation itself was sufficient to justify a homeowner's motives. By 1965, 200,000 shelters had been built.

PERIPHERAL AND CENTRAL ROUTES

In the early years of psychological analysis, two competing versions of human behavior emerged. On the one hand, the rise of densely populated urban centers paired with the arts of advertising and mass politics created an image of human beings in crowds as driven by irrational impulses and raw feelings. On the other hand, studies that actually examined individual decision-making often found people to make perfectly rational decisions in their own self-interest. Why the difference? The answer, finally formalized in what is today called the Elaboration Likelihood Model, was that the human mind had two "pathways" for decision-making. The first pathway, called the **peripheral route**, always takes the quickest shortcut based on simple cues. The second pathway, called the **central route**, uses complex reasoning and careful investigation to compare and contrast alternatives before arriving at a decision. And since every individual would make use of both pathways, sometimes using one and sometimes using the other, the same individual that appeared irrational and impulsive in one situation would turn around and seem completely rational and deliberate in another. What mattered was the "likelihood" in any situation that the mind would choose "elaboration" (the central route) because it deemed the choice important.

What determines a person's preference of the central route over the peripheral route? There are two factors involved in this choice. The first is **motivation**, which means a desire to exert energy and overcome resistance to produce an outcome that is deemed important for the person's well-being. Motivation is thus more than a liking, a craving, or a wish. It is more like a drive, an ambition, or necessity. When a stimulus is perceived by perceptual judgment as relating to some core need or desire of the person, the mind's decision making process tends to shift toward the central route. Anything that seems trivial or unrelated to those interests, or alternatively that is considered straightforward and unproblematic, takes the peripheral route. The second factor is **ability**, which means not only the personal skills, knowledge, and resources a person possesses, but also the time, circumstances, and opportunity to fully consider one's options. Sometimes, therefore, a person must use peripheral route processing if they are forced to make snap judgments under pressure or simply have no resources to use or to consult in making a decision. And resources also include not being exhausted. Just think of how much energy we expend when faced with resolving health issues in ourselves or our loved ones, the financial stress of debt, bills and investments, relationship conflicts between family and friends, or the many responsibilities we have at our jobs. When we are literally worn out by all of the "serious" matters we face every day, no wonder that we just take mental shortcuts for all of the other thousand judgments we must make that seem minor or distant from our "serious" concerns.

We often see each of these two routes being used by the same groups to reach different audiences. For instance, an activist group fighting for climate justice called Extinction Rebellion UK tries to exploit every avenue of persuasion in its campaign to fight global warming and its environmental impacts. On the one hand, it uses central route persuasion by organizing what they call "community assemblies," which consist of "local people hearing, deliberating and deciding about local issues that affect community lives every day." Volunteers have access to a "Community Assembly Manual" and are given instructions and resources to contact local councils and municipal authorities as well as tactics for more aggressive tactics of taking over buildings and demanding change. These actions require heavy investments of time and resources as well as an in-depth knowledge of the problem and potential solutions.[5] On the other hand, the group is well known for its creative and daring protests that make use of different art forms to capture public attention. One street protest, for instance, featured a group known as the "Red Rebels" (because of their all-red dress and striking white-painted faces) who captured press coverage by standing in front of a bewildered line of police, their palms open in front of them as if in supplication, as if they were otherworldly beings. These peripheral route tactics rely on graphic, easily understandable symbolism to dramatize a situation of crisis to capture public attention without dwelling on the details of the problem.[6]

As this example shows, central route messaging cannot exploit the same persuasive tools as peripheral route tactics. It simply relies on effective argumentation and reasoning. Therefore it is fair to conclude that any message functions *as* propaganda only within peripheral route reprocessing. For instance, an object created by an actual propagandist, for instance a World War II poster, does not function *as* propaganda when it is studied as a historical object. Propaganda functions as propaganda only when it functions to simplify ideas and stimulate a reflex action in a distracted mass audience. The moment that serious, critical inquiry begins, propaganda loses its capacity to influence. This is also the reason why it is easier to see the flaws in an opponent's propaganda than in one's own. It is not because the other side is populated with dupes. Rather, because we agree with the conclusions of the messages we consume, we do not spend much effort investigating its contradictions. But a critic, energized to expose what they see to be manipulations and lies, will go to great lengths to reveal them. The idealistic conclusion we often come to is that everyone at all times should employ central reprocessing when consuming messages. But this is to ask the impossible. We rely on propaganda precisely because it would take a year to thoroughly investigate every message that we might see in a single week. The demand that we correct the limits of humanity by being superhuman is hardly a solution to the problem of being human. Often we simply need to trust that other people know what they are talking about so we can expend energy on our own pressing issues. We must approach propaganda with an attitude of realism concerning what is within our power to genuinely achieve.

REFLEXES

In 1959, when the threat of a nuclear strike by the Soviet Union seemed not only possible but imminent, people began focusing on the very real threat of "fallout radiation." Consequently, Section II of the pamphlet is appropriately titled "You Can Protect Yourself from Fallout Radiation." The term triggered a flight and shelter response, as once fallout radiation got into the atmosphere, there was little one could do to avoid it, as the pamphlet's weather pattern charts made vividly clear. The only thing you could do was to hide behind brick walls and wait it out. As the pamphlet explains, "Any mass of material between you and the fallout will cut down the amount of radiation that reaches you. Sufficient mass will make you safe." The government wanted the fear of fallout radiation to become so pervasive that it would become a reflex. If people heard it was approaching, they would know exactly what to do.

It was a reasonable strategy. The vast majority of our experiences and behavior, in fact, is determined by our body of reflexes, instinctive or acquired, that orient us to the objects, events, and people of our world. A **reflex** is a patterned response to recognizable stimuli that satisfies some immediate impulse. A "patterned response" is something akin to a habit that combines elements of cognition, emotion, and action within a familiar sequence. These responses range from an almost purely instinctive reflexive jumping and surprise to more complex responses such as the reflex to hold the door open for strangers or to prefer ordering only nonfat lattes. A "recognizable stimuli" are those specific and familiar experiences that trigger reflexes when we enter into both familiar and unfamiliar situations. Lastly, reflexes are not simply irrational, knee-jerk reactions to stimuli that are akin to a billiard ball striking a bumper. Reflexes "satisfy some immediate impulse" insofar as they are often practically motivated and developed to accomplish some aim, even if the aim is simply pleasure or avoidance. Reflexes are thus part of motives because they immediately "size up" parts of our environment and tell us how to act within it. Reflexes thus often serve to smooth our way into, or out of, social situations. They tell us immediately what is desirable and what should be avoided and how to react to either one.

In Italy, for instance, the traditional practices of cooking and dining were disrupted by the opening of a McDonald's restaurant near the Spanish Steps in Rome in 1986. Many Italians took offense at the presence of an American fast food restaurant at such an iconic location, with some critics seeing it as a threat of "Americanization" of Italian culture. One Italian journalist, Carlo Petrini, attempted to create a new set of reflexes to preserve traditional Italian cuisine. First, to protest the opening of the McDonald's, he organized a convivial event distributing a pasta dish in the piazza in front of the restaurant to emphasize the difference between genuine Italian food and homogeneously mass-produced hamburgers. His intention was to crystallize a reflex against anything perceived as "fast food," investing the McDonald's logo in particular with highly negative connotations.[7] Second, he initiated what he called a "Slow Food" movement that would celebrate the long-standing practices of food cultivation, preparation, and dining that characterized Italian cuisine. To create an easily identifiable stimulus, he invented a snail logo (called the "Snail of Approval") that would be given to food establishments that had shown dedication to attending to food sourcing, environmental impact, cultural connection, community involvement, staff support, and business values.[8] Petrini thus hoped that consumers would develop reflexes that would patronize any business with a snail logo while shunning fast food companies.

MYTH

One of the remarkable characteristics of the "Family Fallout Shelter" pamphlet is the way it narrates the catastrophe of the hypothetical nuclear strike. After acknowledging that the targets of the strikes would be air and missile bases, it goes on to make some vague and ominous claims: "The enemy would try to knock out our retaliatory power. He might also try to destroy our cities. Nobody can be sure now how far the enemy will go." Although the Soviet Union is clearly assumed to be the source of the strikes, nowhere in the document is any actual foreign government named. Instead, it talks of "the enemy" who is personified by the pronoun "he" as if the source of nuclear strikes was a single malicious person (or more accurately, demon) in control of awesome tools of violence. The framing of this event invites US citizens to see themselves as victims of some nameless Evil who seeks to control the world and devastate all who oppose Him. And if citizens must heroically endure suffering by surviving nuclear fallout in their homemade shelters, then that is the price to pay for the inevitable triumph of Justice.

Myths like this are one of the essential organizing principles of all large-scale and enduring propaganda. Although directing reflexes is the ultimate goal of all propaganda, reflexes themselves are too diverse, inconsistent, and ephemeral to constitute an enduring motive. It would be costly and exhausting for any propagandist to keep track of and guide every single relevant reflex as if it were an isolated stimulus and response. What is required is to organize and make sense of our reflexes into a loosely coherent whole that remains largely the same across different contexts. This function is performed by myth. Even when we think we are often responding rationally to discrete stimuli in a specific context, we are often playing out the implications of a myth. The myths that we internalize often function as the constants of our personality and worldview across different periods of our lives and only shift when something dramatic has happened in our lives to overturn them. While reflexes must constantly adapt to every new phenomenon in our lives, from judging the latest version of the smartphone to the campaign platform of the latest presidential candidate, our myths simply endure.

A **myth** is a sweeping narrative of origins and destinies that provides enduring models of action and value that are recurrent over time and which potentially answer all questions in vague but emotionally satisfying ways. A good myth explains where we came from and where we are going. One can think of the most widely shared myths as having general enough forms to be identified with a single word. The myths of Progress, Decline, Work, Freedom, Salvation, Heroism, Martyrdom, Revolution, Apocalypse, Survival, Discovery, or Home can all be rendered as a simple plot formula. For instance, the myth of Freedom sees the current state of oppression, inequality, and restriction as temporary evils that will eventually be overcome through struggle so that, in the end, every person will be able to live as they wish without limitation or constraint. The myth of Home, by contrast, says that although children will always wander away to discover and try new things, eventually the family finds happiness only by returning to the same place of its birth and nurturing. In the case of the "Family Fallout Shelter," the myth of Survival tells us that even when catastrophe might wipe out most of known civilization, it is imperative that the survivors must live on so that civilization can start anew. Propaganda uses these myths by making them more specific. A free-market economic policy may result in economic inequality, but the myth of the American Dream guarantees that with ingenuity and effort anyone can succeed. And a nationalistic propaganda of a small country that has suffered emigration, but is trying to call back its diaspora to its native land, might use a propaganda that instructs an inspiring image that uses the myth of Home.

A common myth that global technology companies use to justify the development and usage of any and all innovations, for instance, is that of "Progress," specifically *technological* progress. Within this myth, which can be traced back to the Greek myth of Prometheus, human beings were given the ability to create amazing inventions that would act as tools for crafting new and better civilizations. But this myth also can explain the ways that inventions also have threatened civilizations, most namely through war. Human frailty always can misuse technology, leading to suffering, but ultimately it is human creativity that will solve the problems created by innovation itself.[9] For instance, when the development of the first functional artificial intelligence program, called ChatGPT, was released by OpenAI in 2022, people were amazed but also terrified by the new innovation. But OpenAI CEO Sam Altman remained optimistic, believing that AI will not only become more capable but more ubiquitous: "People are using it to create amazing things. If we could see what each of us can do 10 or 20 years in the future, it would astonish us today," he told an interviewer.[10] In the myth of Progress, any innovation may have short-term negative consequences, but over time it will become a necessary and essential part of human life. Rather than fight against technology, therefore, the myth tells us, as all myths do, that we must embrace it because it is necessary and inevitable.

COMPENSATORY SUBSTITUTES

Perhaps the most controversial legacy of one of the founders of twentieth-century propaganda, the public relations specialist Edward Benays, was his notion of "compensatory substitutes." Bernays was a nephew of Sigmund Freud and was highly influenced by his uncle's theory of psychoanalysis. Freud had posited that despite our self-understanding as rational beings, humans were actually propelled by irrational drives that we often suppressed or "sublimated" into socially acceptable practices. For Bernays, the outlet for these sublimated desires was called a **compensatory substitute**, which is that object that sells a product, policy, or practice by arousing a basic desire which we were ashamed to admit that we possessed and then providing, in its place, a socially acceptable vehicle by which that desire might be satisfied. Bernays thus sought to profit from our different types of neurosis. For instance, whereas Freud might have provided therapies for men who had an Oedipus complex that made them want to kill their father, Bernays might have suggested that it would be more profitable to try selling new suits to sons that would show them to be more fashionable and thereby more successful than their fathers—thus "killing" them with better style.

Another foundation of Bernays's "new propaganda" (so-called in the 1920s) was that of exploiting the "group mind," something he believed that psychoanalytic techniques had discovered in opposition to the individualistic psychologies of the nineteenth century. What Bernays meant by the **group mind** was not an alternative or collective consciousness, but rather our conception of what other people feel and think that guides our decision-making practices. The group mind thus subordinated instrumental rationality to the satisfaction of social desires. The motives categorized under the group mind would thus include competitiveness, sexuality, aesthetic pleasure, gregariousness, ambition, vindictiveness, aggression, possessiveness, cooperativeness, altruism, and exhibitionism. The group mind thus refers to a certain mental attitude that grows out of our association with others, creates a coherent picture of that social environment by attributing certain shared qualities to a particular group, evaluates one's standing in relationship to that group, and then judges the possible benefits or detriments to that relationship that comes from adopting some practice or using some product. The appeal to the group mind is simply to say that a good part of human motivation is social in nature. In today's marketing environment, this hardly amounts to the revelation that it was in the 1920s. Products of all kinds, from soap to smartphones to cars to produce, are sold by presenting attractive images of the social environment in which they are associated with sometimes little else to recommend them.

Motives inspired by the group mind thus are different than those which function as compensatory substitutes. First, the group mind tactic is wholly transparent. One might sell beer, for instance, by showing close friends sharing a beer. From the perspective of the group mind, it is not the taste or quality of the beer itself that is advertised, but its ability to satisfy the gregarious instinct. Group mind appeals are completely up-front about this fact. Second, there is nothing "shameful" in the desires of the group mind. Everyone wants friends, for instance, and if sharing a beer is a way to solidify friendship, then all the better. A compensatory substitute, in con-tradistinction, begins with a typically problematic desire and often does not admit how that desire is being satisfied. Because in its raw form (at least in the original theory) the desire that motivates a compensatory substitute cannot be admitted or expressed in polite society, a replacement must be created that renames and redirects the samples into a different, more acceptable, form. A young man, for instance, may feel sexually inadequate or bullied by his peers. He craves sexual and physical conquest. Along comes an advertisement for a 4×4 truck demonstrating raw power. The truck becomes a way of "compensating" for the young man's perceived inadequacies (whether real or imagined) and thus the truck appears worth the price, despite the fact that the purchaser has absolutely no need for such an off-road vehicle in the city.

For instance, one of the lasting gender stereotypes that exploits compensatory substitutes is the connection between outdoor grill-ing and masculinity. A product of the 1950s suburban culture that was a conscious invention of the marketing industry, the image of the man mastering his grill while ruling over the people gathered in his backyard is ingrained in popular culture. In a 2010 *Forbes* article, writer Meghan Casserly lists three of the reasons why grill-ing satisfies the suppressed desires of men. First, grilling acts as a compensatory substitute for desiring to do something exciting and dangerous: "You've got lighter fluid, a match, a breeze and a miniature pitchfork to stab things with." Second, grilling satisfies the group mind by creating an all-male social space: "The grill provides entertainment for the men, who tend to congregate around it, usually with beers." Lastly, grilling does not require much cleaning, thus satisfying a practical need to not have to do much labor.[11] A recent survey done in Wales found that almost half of respondents believed grilling was the exclusive responsibility of men, with only 1% believing it was the domain of women.[12] Not surprisingly, the propaganda of the grill as a compensatory substitute also creates a constant incentive for men to purchase larger grills.

COGNITIVE DISSONANCE

One of the unique consequences of being a symbol-using animal is the desire to maintain a consistent and coherent image of oneself. People can tolerate chaos and inconsistency in the world around them. But chaos and inconsistency within themselves, at least over time, becomes intolerable—or, to put it more specifically, the *feeling* of chaos and inconsistency becomes intolerable. For one could say, with good reason, that chaos and inconsistency is simply the law of being human. Faced with so many different situations and embedded in so many diverse relationships, we may find it natural that contradictions and tensions arise between our attitudes, beliefs, and practices across time and context. Most of the time, however, we live largely unaware of these tensions. We simply adapt to the situation at hand and move on. But there are moments in which these contradictions are made salient, usually in situations involving conflict, controversy, or argument, and we feel the need to account for ourselves. It is during these situations in which we experience the painful side effects of hypocrisy, deceptiveness, cowardice, disloyalty, betrayal, or ignorance. Perhaps we claim to believe in a principle but fail to uphold it, make a promise but then fail to follow through, condemn an action but then do it oneself, praise a virtue but then commit the vice, or state one thing to a person's face but then say another behind their back. All of these actions are socially frowned upon and evoke discomfort in the one acting.

This experience of discomfort is called cognitive dissonance, which propaganda exploits through the rationalization trap. **Cognitive dissonance** is this feeling of discomfort that results from holding two contradictory ideas in one's mind that have a bearing on one's own self-image. By an **idea** I mean a simple statement of fact. Sets of opposing ideas might include "I am honest" ↔ "I just lied," or "I am health conscious" ↔ "I smoke cigarettes," or "You are a good friend" ↔ "I didn't invite you to my birthday party," or "Killing is wrong" ↔ "I support the death penalty." In each case, we have an apparent contradiction that at least, on its face, demands some kind of accounting. The **rationalization trap** then deliberately arouses cognitive dissonance and then provides a rationalization for resolving that dissonance that serves the interests of the propagandist (and, presumably, the one experiencing cognitive dissonance as well). The rationalization trap follows two basic steps. First, it makes the target emotionally and cognitively aware of a contradiction between two ideas in order to create discomfort. Second, it provides an easy and manageable way to resolve this dissonance that is satisfying to the target and also benefits the propagandist. Propaganda is thus presented as serving an almost therapeutic purpose. Imagine, for instance, the methods of making "interventions" for people with substance abuse problems. Usually such encounters rely on the dissonance of the two sets of ideas, one set being "I love my family" ↔ "I am hurting my family," the other being "I desire to have a future" ↔ "I am destroying my future." By creating a social environment in which this dissonance is made salient and unavoidable, the preferred way of resolving dissonance—going to rehabilitation therapy—looks attractive and necessary.

But rationalization traps need not be so serious. They are often very simple and may even produce a sense of laughter and satisfaction. For instance, in 2023, the restaurant chain Chili's released an ad campaign with the slogan "You Deserve Them More Than Kids Do." The ad featured a woman in business attire interviewing children as if they were employees at a company—only with a basket of chicken crispers between them. The interviews included questions like "Do you worry about your credit score?" or "Have you not been able to fall asleep because you are worried about getting enough sleep?" or "Have you ever tried to split the bill at a large group dinner when someone had only a 'few bites' of the appetizer?" The children, of course, have no frame of reference to these questions because they do not deal with adult problems (except for the question "What do you do during summer break?" which elicited the answer "I tickle my sister"). The slogan only appears at the end of the commercial without explanation, but it actually completes a rationalization trap. Parents are well-known for treating their children with fried chicken meals and denying themselves the same reward. The ad challenges this practice with two sets of dissonant ideas, "The children did no work" ↔ "The children deserve a treat" and "Adults work hard" ↔ "Adults don't treat themselves." By showing how children have no conception of adult responsibilities, the commercial proves that it is the parents, not the children, who should be eating the chicken crispers as a reward for all the sacrifices they make to work and raise a family.[13]

But behavior change is not always the end result of the rationalization trap. Often, it is used to justify pre-existing beliefs and habits and to resist the pressure to change. Much propaganda, in fact, deliberately arouses dissonance precisely to make people even more committed to the status quo. This type is often found expressed by pundits and partisan news broadcasts, and often starts with phrases like "some people are saying" or "they want you to believe" or "they accuse you of being" in order to arouse dissonance before they then proceed to provide a way of resolving it. The goal here is to exaggerate some attack by a perceived critic who wishes to arouse dissonance for the purposes of change and then to refute this perceived attack by providing an even more airtight justification to continue doing, thinking, and believing the same exact thing. The emotions used here are usually a combination of resentment and indignation. Indeed, the majority of rationalizations are precisely of this type for the very reason that people rarely need much of an excuse not to change. And the benefit is that this form of propaganda makes them feel self-righteous for doing so while keeping them firmly committed to consuming the propaganda.

There are six strategies of resolving cognitive dissonance.

Change

The most direct response to cognitive dissonance is simply **change**, which is to choose one idea and reject the other. Change does not simply mean doing something new. It means to give up something old. For instance, a common appeal to change in our daily lives deals with habits of diet. Because everyone must consume food and drink every day, enormous energy is invested by propagandists to get us to "give up" one thing and "start" another. The tactic is to present simple dichotomies and to present one as being consistent with values and the other inconsistent. If you care about the environment, you should stop buying mass-produced foods and eat organic. If you want better digestion, you should choose gluten-free pasta and give up bread. If you are serious about losing weight, you need to give up carbs and eat only meat and protein. Appeals to change are often not very subtle. They exaggerate differences and eliminate any middle ground, thus forcing a dramatic choice. But appeals to change risk sparking a backlash if too strong. When there is no middle ground, this can result in a form of polarization. For instance, a provocative ad produced by PETA (People for the Ethical Treatment of Animals) shows a young girl saying "grace" at Thanksgiving, only to have her express thanks for all of the cruel ways that turkeys are treated on their way to the dinner table. The cognitive dissonance produced by the ideas "I am an ethical person" ↔ "I support the torture of animals" is designed to encourage giving up meat altogether in order to restore one's self-image.[14] But this type of approach also makes compromise virtually impossible.

Denial

The opposite tactic of change is denial, at least to the extent that one can call this a tactic. **Denial** is an effort to deny that cognitive dissonance exists by simply blocking out any messages that would emphasize that dissonance. Put simply, denial plugs one's ears. This can be accomplished by not listening to sources that would remind one of this dissonance, either by tuning out certain media or by literally cutting oneself off from communication with other people. Denial is therefore a form of isolation. If one never encounters anything that brings to light the contradiction, then that contradiction is not felt to exist. Today, people can accomplish this by retreating into an "echo chamber" that consists only of those who repeat the same set of closed ideas and are not open to alternatives. The result, in extreme cases, is a kind of denialism that prevents people from encountering opposing views. Media critic Eli Pariser, for instance, coined the term "filter bubble" to refer to the way that algorithms even modify the content of internet searches to conform to the history and preferences of the user, calling it a "personal ecosystem of information" that insulates people "from any sort of cognitive dissonance by limiting what we see."[15] And because many sites offer personalized content based on our browsing history and other data, the result is a constant blocking out of any views that would arouse any doubt or contradiction.

Bolstering

A weak but prevalent form of rationalization is bolstering, which is not so much a way of resolving the contradiction as it is of drowning it out with applause. **Bolstering** accepts the contradiction but appeals to the conventions of one's surroundings and especially one's favorite peer group. It amounts to the defense of "sure, but everyone else is doing it." Bolstering simply throws up one's hands at the contradiction and accepts it as it is, at least as long as one is surrounded by a supportive social environment. One finds bolstering especially in situations in which a person is exposed to peer pressure and groupthink. Add drugs and alcohol to the mix, and soon people are engaging in actions they swore they would never do. But as long as they are surrounded by others doing the same thing, then everything seems okay, at least for a while. But bolstering is short-lived, lasting only so long as the supportive atmosphere exists close at hand. To borrow the metaphor of the party, the hangover the next morning always brings regret and the dissonance rushes backs in. Bolstering can lead to a self-destructive cycle in which one only feels justified when one is amidst that group, but when outside the group produces forms of self-hatred. Bolstering allows us to get along in society but at the expense of keeping the underlying dissonance festering behind the scenes. For instance, normally it would be a sign of reckless irresponsibility to put oneself willingly in danger by running alongside angry bulls that could potentially gorge a person and kill them with its horns. But in the festival of San Fermin in Pamplona, Spain, such activity is allowed and in fact encouraged during the famous "Running of the Bulls" held every July. Immortalized in literature by Ernest Hemingway in *The Sun Also Rises*, the festival today attracts thousands of tourists eager to put themselves in danger, rationalized by the appeal to "tradition" that licenses such behavior during the week of the festival.[16] How could it be wrong if it has been a Spanish tradition for over 400 years?

Modification

Unlike bolstering, which merely pushes the contradiction into the background, modification actually seeks to dissolve it entirely by altering the terms of the contradiction. **Modification** entails altering the premises and facts of one or both sides in order to show that there is, in fact, no actual contradiction. When the changes to the premises involve misleading manipulation of facts, modification can be characterized as **distortion**, as when the petroleum industry might deny global warming in order to justify its continued investment in fossil fuels. But modification need not always involve distortion. It simply means changing the accepted terms of the contradiction to something new. Even an action or belief that appears to contradict scientific findings can be rationalized if future research reveals the initial scientific findings to be inaccurate. When the first smallpox vaccines were tested, for instance, it would have seemed absurd to most people to protect oneself from a virus by exposing oneself to it. Modification, in short, often relies on gathering information, usually from sources one finds credible, in order to alter the facts of the case and show that an apparent contradiction is an illusion (even if one's interpretation of what constitutes "credibility" may be highly suspect). For instance, in 2020 fires were burning thousands of acres of Amazonian rainforest in Brazil, but then–President Jair Bolsonaro rejected claims that he was failing to protect his nation's land. In a speech to the United Nations, he not only falsely claimed that the fires were restricted to the very edges of the forest, but he also falsely blamed indigenous peoples for starting the fires. This distortion of the facts allowed Bolsonaro to appear to be a protector of the Amazon even as he encouraged large-scale land-clearing for cattle grazing.[17]

Differentiation

The tactic of differentiation is more complex than the previous four we have examined. **Differentiation** freely admits the contradiction exists but uses a difference in situational context to explain and justify its existence. It thus makes, as it were, a standing exception to the rule. Imagine, for instance, that one were to state clearly that "Thou shalt not kill" but then attach the qualifier "unless for a just war or for self-defense." This is a pragmatic distinction in context.

Instead of assuming that our principles are universal for all contexts for all times, it states that our principles are active in more limited situations that guarantee dependable outcomes. What seems to be a virtuous action in one context thus appears to be a vice in another. In reality shows like *Survivor*, normally honest, upstanding individuals must engage in constant deception and betrayal in order to win, with the justification being that it is just part of the game. Differentiation thus creates categories of action that seem to stand alone and refuse contradiction. By entering into these situations, differentiation thus either imposes or releases us from obligations that would apply elsewhere. Differentiation thus invites a relativist ethics that looks away from universalist principles and concentrates on the details of circumstance. For instance, when a damaging audio tape was released during the 2016 US presidential campaign that recorded then-candidate Donald Trump making lewd comments about women, he apologized for the remarks but nonetheless rationalized his behavior by calling it "locker room talk." The implication is that although he admitted such behavior was inappropriate for public expression, it was acceptable when surrounded by other men within the private confines of the men's locker room.[18]

Transcendence

Finally, the strategy of transcendence allows us to have it all by transporting us vertically rather than horizontally. The tactic of **transcendence** adopts a position above an apparent contradiction so that it no longer appears to be a contradiction anymore from a perspective of height. In other words, an apparent contradiction can be resolved by adopting a perspective from which they are no longer opposites. Imagine a father who declares unwavering love for his son. And yet every morning during the winter, he wakes him at five in the morning and throws them in an icy lake, only to whip him with a belt when he emerges. How does he reconcile his contradiction? Transcendence: "Life is hard and will abuse you. Only by learning to endure suffering can we achieve greatness." Transcendence allows the father both to be loving and cruel and be proud of both. This move to a "higher" justification is called upward transcendence because it makes an apparent problematic action a praiseworthy one. Actions that are done "for the greater good" or "for the glory of God" or "in sacrifice for freedom" are all arguments from transcendence. When Russian president Vladimir Putin ordered the invasion of Ukraine in February 2022, for instance, his justifications immediately presented a paradox. On the one hand, Putin claimed that Ukraine was a part of Russia and that Ukrainians and Russians were one people. On the other hand, his invasion created the conditions for the wholesale destruction of cities and the deaths of tens of thousands of Ukrainians. Putin resolved this dissonance by claiming that "Nazis" had taken over the Ukrainian state and were committing "genocide" against nature Russians, so that the invasion would "denazify" Ukraine and therefore liberate the people. Despite fighting a war with Ukraine, Putin could nonetheless see himself as the protector of Ukrainians.[19]

WHY NO ONE IS A SHEEP

Everything people do, they do because of a reason they believe is good and that will empower them in some way. From an outside perspective, of course, people seem to act irrationally, self-destructively, cruelly, and immorally all the time. But one of the most important things for propagandists and critics alike to always keep in mind is that individuals are not dupes. Everyone has a reason for what they believe in what they do, an image of themselves as a rational, moral being, and a desire to assert their will in the world. No matter one's class, education, nationality, gender, race, ethnicity, or any other demographic category, all human individuals wish to develop one's capacities to act and to achieve aims in the recalcitrant universe. No one is a "sheep" and no one wishes to "follow" and "obey" or be "passive" and "mindless." But that impression, more often than not, is created by propaganda itself in cooperation with our own pride. Nothing guarantees, empirically speaking, that any social action will produce good outcomes. And many good intentions are guided by misconceptions that result in disaster. Despite all of this, to understand why people do what they do, it is best to assume they believe what they are doing is justified and in their best interests. Propaganda gives them such justifications.

This chapter has outlined some of the foundations of human motivation that are used by propaganda to alter beliefs and behavior. We begin with the awareness that our aims and reasons grow out of our conception of the situation in which we are immersed, and that our moral and practical disagreements more often than not grow out of our different conceptions of the situation. Propaganda provides descriptions of the situations that simplify conditions and encourage certain paths of action. Propaganda is most influential when it addresses individuals in a mass context, when they are hurried, distracted, and immersed in a crowd. These appeals cater to the peripheral route processing by providing simple cues for understanding and response. By creating a credible image of authority, by presenting dramatic narratives that arouse emotions, by appealing to basic inferential logics, these messages direct interest and attention to those matters of concern to the propagandist. For instance, by using these tactics, the US government convinced 200,000 citizens to build what turned out to be completely useless concrete bunkers in their backyards in the name of national security.

But propaganda is not just about the "product." Propaganda constructs an entire symbolic environment that invites its target audience to accept it as a representation of reality. Within these representations, people see themselves as members of different social groups, each with its own mind. The audience is thus invited to see themselves as being a part of the social group and to judge matters from the group mind perspective. And in a more subtle way, propaganda can also provide compensatory substitutes for impulses and desires we refuse to admit to ourselves, but which may be provided as a vehicle for expression welcomed by that same social group. Lastly, propaganda makes use of tensions within ourselves or between other people, arousing cognitive dissonance in order to generate the tension needed for action. By arousing these tensions and providing outlets for their resolution, propaganda creates rationalization traps that channel behavior into desired pathways. Once enacted, they then hope that it becomes a habit that can be relied upon for quantifiable outcomes. This is the world of propaganda in which we live. And no one is an exception to the rule. We are all subject to the same appeals and susceptible to the same reactions. To assume that one is immune is, ironically, to make oneself all the more susceptible. Nothing is more exploitable than pride. Like any addiction, we learn to master propaganda's influence by first admitting that we often feel we cannot do without it.

DISCUSSION QUESTIONS

1. Discussions of the peripheral and central routes often present the latter in a positive light and the former in a negative one. Consider, for the sake of argument, situations in which adopting the central route would actually be the wrong choice and the peripheral route be preferred. How does propaganda make use of these situations?

2. In what aspects of our lives do we often experience cognitive dissonance the most often? In what ways does propaganda target this aspect of our lives to intentionally generate cognitive dissonance, and what pathways of change do they offer to resolve it? By contrast, does propaganda exist that offers ways of resolving this dissonance without change?

EXERCISES

1. Consider some of the objects in which we invest considerable importance, such as our smartphones or cars. If you were creating a new campaign for one of these products that was intentionally provocative, how would you make use of compensatory substitutes to sell it? Could you also make use of cognitive dissonance in this campaign?

2. Find speeches by leaders in a military conflict, whether they are Presidents, insurgents, or revolutionaries. How do they use myths to justify violence? What are the differences between the myths used by representatives of established states and those used by those trying to overturn them?

SUGGESTED READINGS

For a discussion of the psychology of propaganda and its reliance on reflex and myth, there is no better resource than Jacques Ellul's *Propaganda: The Formation of Men's Attitudes*. In my opinion the best book ever written on the subject from a sociological perspective, Ellul presents propaganda as both a modern necessity and a method of producing mass neurosis.

At this point it is essential to read Edward Bernays's *Propaganda*, which established most of the foundations of modern public relations. This short book will be useful not only for its psychology but for its focus on creating events, which will be shown in the next chapter.

Lastly, the *Age of Propaganda: The Everyday Use and Abuse of Persuasion* by Anthony Pratkanis and Elliot Aronson presents not only a succinct review of the peripheral route processing as well as cognitive dissonance, but also will be a useful resource for many of the tactics described in the rest of this book.

NOTES

1 Office of Civil and Defense Mobilization, "The family fallout shelter," Prelinger Library: San Francisco, 2008. https://www.survivorlibrary.com/library/the_family_fallout_shelter_1959.pdf.

2 Mia Jankowicz, "The coronavirus outbreak has prompted people around the world to panic buy toilet paper. Here's why," *Business Insider*, March 10, 2020, https://www.businessinsider.com/coronavirus-panic-buying-toilet-paper-stockpiling-photos-2020-3.

3 Armani Syed, "Why protesters are squirting water at tourists in Barcelona," *Time*, July 8, 2024, https://time.com/6995756/barcelona-protesters-water-pistols-tourists/.

4 "Nude calendar stunt helps pave Sask. highway," *CBC News*, November 5, 2010, https://www.cbc.ca/news/canada/saskatchewan/nude-calendar-stunt-helps-pave-sask-highway-1.963358.

5 "Community assemblies escalation plan," Extinction Rebellion, https://extinctionrebellion.uk/act-now/campaigns/community-assemblies-escalation-plan/.

6 Anna Behrmann, "The artists of Extinction Rebellion: 'Our bold imagery is helping to change the conversations around climate change'," *i*, November 24, 2019, https://inews.co.uk/culture/arts/extinction-rebellion-artist-protest-banner-art-red-rebel-flag-logo-366404?srsltid=AfmBOoopEuNc i5pBaUQwt33LewsJCwFUQaei_ZDxW8l5JA7un7yFZH66.

7 Sarah van Gelder, "'Slow Food' pioneer's love for food ripened into a life's work," United Nations University, June 1, 2016, https://ourworld.unu.edu/en/slow-food-pioneers-love-for-food-ripened-into-a-lifes-work.

8 "Snail of Approval," Slow Food USA, https://slowfoodusa.org/snail-of-approval/.

9 Rose Eveleth, "The biggest lie tech people tell themselves—and the rest of us," *Vox*, October 8, 2019, https://www.vox.com/the-highlight/2019/10/1/20887003/tech-technology-evolution-natural-inevitable-ethics.

10 Brian Eastwood, "Sam Altman believes AI will change the world (and everything else)," MIT Sloan School of Management, May 8, 2024, https://mitsloan.mit.edu/ideas-made-to-matter/sam-altman-believes-ai-will-change-world-and-everything-else.

11 Meghan Casserly, "Grilling, guys and the great gender divide," *Forbes*, July 19, 2013, https://www.forbes.com/2010/07/01/grilling-men-women-barbecue-forbes-woman-time-cooking.html.

12 Neil Shaw, Why barbecuing is still seen as a man's job," *Wales Online*, May 30, 2023, https://www.walesonline.co.uk/whats-on/food-drink-news/barbecuing-still-seen-mans-job-27019484.

13 "Chili's is launching a new campaign created by Mischief called 'You Deserve Them More Than Kids Do'," Ads of Brands, September 18, 2023, https://adsofbrands.net/en/news/chili%E2%80%99s-is-launching-a-new-campaign-created-by-mischief-called-you-deserve-them-more-than-kids-do/5042.

14 "Grace: peta2's Thanksgiving ad," PETA, https://www.peta.org/videos/grace-peta2s-thanksgiving-ad/.

15 "How filter bubbles distort reality: everything you need to know," Farnam Street, https://fs.blog/filter-bubbles/.

16 "Quick Guide. What is the Running of the Bulls," SanFermin.com, https://www.sanfermin.com/en/running-of-the-bulls/quick-guide-what-is-the-running-of-the-bulls/.

17 "In speech at the UN, Bolsonaro plays down environmental crisis and disregards secularism," Conectas, https://www.conectas.org/en/noticias/in-speech-at-the-un-bolsonaro-plays-down-environmental-crisis-and-disregards-secularism/.

18 Danielle Diaz, "3 times Trump defended his 'locker room' talk," CNN, October 9, 2016, https://www.cnn.com/2016/10/09/politics/donald-trump-locker-room-talk-presidential-debate-2016-election/index.html.

19 Rachel Treisman, "Putin's claim of fighting against Ukraine 'neo-Nazis' distorts history, scholars say," NPR, March 1, 2022, https://www.npr.org/2022/03/01/1083677765/putin-denazify-ukraine-russia-history.

CREATING EVENTS

The front page of *The New York Times* of April 1, 1929 featured a column running down the full length of the left side of the page. Titled "Easter Sun Finds the Past in Shadow at Modern Parade," the column featured a mosaic of impressions from the reporter. Perhaps the most notable sign of change was indicated by one of the subtitles: "Group of Girls Puff at Cigarettes as a Gesture of 'Freedom'." A description then followed in the second paragraph: "A group of young women, who said they were smashing a tradition and not preferring any particular brand, strolled along the lane between the tiered skyscrapers and puffed cigarettes." At the time this article was published, women smoking in public was largely absent and even explicitly banned because cigarettes were seen as an exclusively masculine practice. So when a small group of fashionable young women decided to light up cigarettes at the Easter parade, it made headlines for "smashing a tradition" and symbolizing the transition to the "modern." The reporter had found something worth writing about that would grab the attention of his readers.[1]

Although a seemingly incidental detail that had simply caught the attention of the reporter, these lines were the end result of a carefully crafted propaganda campaign designed by Edward Bernays. He had been hired by the American Tobacco Company to market cigarettes to women, but he realized he could not simply target them directly without sparking a backlash. Instead, he had to create a media event that would suggest a different way of framing the issue. After consulting famed psychoanalysis Dr. A. A. Brill, Bernays based

DOI: 10.4324/9781003607236-3

his campaign on the idea that cigarettes might serve as compensatory substitutes for women's suppressed desire for what was then considered a form of male power. To do this, Bernays connected the issue of women smoking to the larger fight for gender equality. First, he got the contact information for 30 debutantes from a friend at *Vogue* magazine and telegrammed them to encourage their participation in the demonstration. Second, he created a cliché for the act of rebellion by re-labelling the cigarettes as "torches of freedom," thus connecting a woman smoking to the Statue of Liberty. Finally, Bernays contacted reporters from all the major newspapers, alerting them to the anticipated act of social protest and providing the narrative around which the event would be framed. When the reporter described their lighting up of cigarettes as "smashing a tradition" and making a "gesture of 'freedom'," he was using the language given to him by Bernays. But the reporter used this language not because he was on the payroll of the American Tobacco Company, but for the simple reason that the framing device Bernays had provided made for a good story.

This classic example of early 20th-century propaganda demonstrates that mass persuasion is about more than crafting and disseminating messages. It also seeks to produce real objects, actions, and events in the world that can function as levers of influence. Consider, for instance, commonly recognized events created explicitly to function as propaganda—the press conference, the grand opening, the sponsored fundraiser, the product release, the political campaign stop, the parade, street protests, the boycott, the terrorist bombing, the convention, the contest, award ceremonies, an act of civil disobedience, or a free concert. All of these events are created to attract media attention and to somehow act as an instigator of change in belief or action. Events give us something objective to talk about that is not simply a reference to what some other people have talked about. To create an event is to make a happening in the world that advances one's own interests. Regretfully, in this case, those interests were purely on the side of the tobacco industry, as those young women who responded to this message of liberation found themselves paying money to become addicted to a health hazard.

What is also remarkable about events like the Easter parade is that often the propagandist does not even have to pay anyone to do or say anything. They merely have to orchestrate events like a good conductor. All of the money and resources went into the design and planning paid to the propagandist by the client. But the actual cost of implementing Bernays's "torches of freedom" was some phone calls, telegrams, and literally a few packages of cigarettes. The rest of the chain of events occurred by the voluntary actions of the participants, each of whom found Bernays's way of framing events to serve their own interests – the debutantes because it satisfied their urge for celebrity and rebellion, the parade because it attracted publicity, and the news reporter because it made for a catchy hook. It is as if Bernays showed evidence of some lost treasure and then provided everyone a map as to how to find it. And even more remarkable still is that the actual designer of these treasure hunts was never identified or made explicit. The primary beneficiary of this campaign (that is, the American Tobacco Company) could simply claim it was at the right place with the right product at the right time. It was the covert nature of creating this event that made it both so effective and so problematic. Readers of the newspaper would never know this was a carefully orchestrated campaign of influence and therefore would not activate their critical faculties as they might do when viewing an advertisement. The case of the "torches of freedom" shows that to understand modern propaganda as something more than rhetoric and persuasion, one must situate the means of persuasion within a modern technological society.

This campaign demonstrated the important of studying what Bernays called "interlocking group formations" that constitutes modern society. **Interlocking group formations** are interconnected networks of social, economic, and political organizations that develop relationships of cooperation and dependency and which also allow individuals to participate in multiple spheres of practice simultaneously. Bernays thus rejected the old 19th-century ideal of the individual acting in isolation with regard to his or her own self-interest—as one might imagine a farmer on the prairie buying a shovel for its durability. Instead, he suggested that we should look at individuals as necessarily interconnected with a variety of overlapping groups while seeing any social practice as being a product of group cooperation. Such an inquiry would document group names, demographics, their interests, aims, and methods, would indicate hierarchies and dependencies, competitors and opponents, would trace supply chains and identify mutual interests, would locate key players that operate as nodes in which many interests intersect, would find active mediators whose job is to establish relationships and negotiate contracts, would determine who designs and passes rules and enforces them, would find events that gather together multiple groups in one place, and would trace the media networks that different groups rely upon. For instance, the success of the "torches of freedom" campaign was due to Bernays's ability to trace social networks. He perceived how "debutantes" stood at the center of fashion, politics, and celebrity while also tracing out the functional relationships amongst *Vogue* magazine, the Easter parade, cigarette companies, *The New York Times*, and the feminist movement. Only by studying interlocking group formations can a propagandist hope to reach an audience without having to directly target it through expensive publicity and marketing. And it is important to note that this method is not restricted to consumer marketing. Social movements, political campaigns, policy debates, the entertainment industry, religious movements, arts and culture advocacy—to name just a few—all can make use of creating events that take advantage of interlocking group formations. Indeed, for groups that lack huge marketing budgets, the ability to create the right event at the right time is an essential way to instigate social change.

This chapter, therefore, will focus on the importance of technique and the structure of our technological society for the development and reception of propaganda. A **technological society** is one marked by the development of industrial, transportation, and communication technologies, the rise in the authority of science and scientific method, the appearance of high-density urban populations, the breakdown of the isolated local community, the increase in mobility and specialization, and the expansion of the power of corporations and the state. Propaganda is misunderstood if it is simply equated with the tactics of manipulation that can be applied in interpersonal contexts. Because propaganda exists only within the context of mass persuasion, it must take into account the structure of mass society. The function is mass persuasion, propaganda must take into account the structure of mass society. For propaganda exists as more than direct messages that are branded with its author and which are explicit in their aim. Much of propaganda comes to us through a chain of different sources that strikes us sometimes without marking itself as propaganda at all. Only by tracing the complex network of relationships and interconnected techniques can we truly understand what differentiates our modern-age propaganda from the rhetorical skill of the classical orators. And only by being aware of these networks can we begin to appreciate just how much of our message-dense environment is deliberate propaganda.

PSEUDO-ENVIRONMENTS

In 1938, CBS radio sponsored a production of *The War of the Worlds*. Based on the novel by H.G. Wells which describes the violent invasion of earth by Martians, the radio script was directed and read by Orson Welles. Notably, the presentation took a very innovative form. Instead of simply reading the story, Welles presented himself as a news broadcaster who would periodically interrupt regularly scheduled music with breaking news stories, each designed to escalate tension. However, some listeners, tuning in late, did not understand the fictional context and took the stories to be real, thus sending them into a panic. The next day, Welles was criticized for irresponsibly misleading the public with media sensationalism. Responding to the public outrage, Wells called a news conference to apologize, in the process making a name for himself as a master storyteller and trickster. Later research found that the level of panic was highly exaggerated, and that the radio program in fact had relatively few listeners. The news media had created a pseudo-environment of widespread mass hysteria that had not, in fact, occurred. The news has constructed one fictional reality to report on another fictional reality, and the result was the creation of an event that still captures our attention and interest.[2]

Coined by the journalist and critic Walter Lippmann, a **pseudo-environment** refers to the picture of the world outside our direct experience that is created through symbols and yet guides action that impacts our actual, lived reality. This stands in contrast to an **environment** which represents the immediate, physical context of one's actions. A pseudo-environment is not, however, the same as simply any fictional universe. The "pseudo" implies an artificial construction that acts as an imitation and replacement of the real. This is why Lippmann associated pseudo-environments with the realm of news, which purports to present what is "actually" happening in the world outside. A child inhabits something like a pseudo-environment only because the borders between reality and fantasy in childhood are fluid. But adults soon develop a clear distinction between pictures of the world they believe they can trust as accurate and those which are lies or designed simply for entertainment. The moment one decides that "this is a picture of the world that is real," that person has chosen their preferred pseudo-environment. The example of *The War of the Worlds* story is thus misleading if it implies that pseudo-environments are *inherently* false, manipulative, or illusory. News reports, documentaries, textbooks, maps, advertisements, novels, encyclopedias, letters, testimony, photographs, satellite images, sonograms, speeches, and paintings are all also used to construct pseudo-environments of the past, present, and the future.

As Lippmann argued, all pseudo-environments are fictions, but that does not mean they are inherently misleading. A **fiction** simply means that something is a symbolic creation that cannot, and can never, be equivalent to what it represents. But all representations have this quality. Even the most accurate map is not equivalent to the landscape it portrays. Fictions are thus more or less valuable as determined by how productively and fruitfully they guide action. We might call a fiction "true," therefore, if it provides a picture of the world on which people can confidently and predictably act, just as following a good set of instructions leads to a successful finished product. Regardless of whether a fiction is a proven scientific theory or the wildest of conspiracy theories, however, it acts as a pseudo-environment to the extent that the person who holds it to be true acts "as if" it was real.

When it comes to the creation of events, therefore, we must always keep in mind that these events, at least when reported by propaganda and not directly witnessed, exist almost entirely in the realm of the pseudo-environment. When people have no direct access to an actual environment in which something exists or has occurred, propaganda can step in and construct a picture of that thing or event that is crafted to engage the emotions, stimulate the imagination, and guide the reason by somehow making these pictures relevant to the experiences and interests of individuals. Sometimes this access is denied because of distance in time or space, as one might think of news dispatches from a foreign war or a historical reconstruction of a battle. Other times it might be inaccessible because of abstraction or scale, as it would be impossible to ever experience a theory of global warming or to actually witness the behavior of viruses or bacteria. Whenever, therefore, we must rely on representations of processes or events we cannot directly experience, we open ourselves up to the potential influence of propaganda.

Propaganda uses its means of persuasion to create events that fit within the pseudo-environments that are comprehensible and interesting to a mass audience. These pseudo-environments create an image of a situation and the events within them that implicate the lives of its audiences, suggesting appropriate forms of action suitable to the situation. Thus, even though pseudo-environments are fictions, the actions people take on the basis of those fictions are very much real. During the COVID-19 pandemic, whether one wore a mask or not, received the vaccine or rejected it, listened to the CDC or preferred the advice of social influencers, believed it was created in a lab or passed naturally from animals, whether there was a government cover-up or a transparent process, all depended on what form of propaganda one preferred.[3] Pseudo-environments may not always match up to reality, but that does not mean they do not have a significant impact on reality. In fact, when people act on the assumptions of their own pseudo-environments, they in turn often serve as instigators of subsequent events—just as a few listeners of the *The War of the Worlds*, believing it was real, were sent into a very real panic for their lives.

CATEGORIES OF PROPAGANDA

Like any communicative genre, propaganda does not come in one form. Unfortunately, in popular entertainment, propaganda tends to be narrowly defined as some overbearing message delivered by a talking head on a giant screen, thanks in large part to George Orwell's *Nineteen Eighty-Four*. But this is only one, and certainly not the most common or effective, category of propaganda. A category of propaganda is an established form, medium, and tenor of communicating that has familiar characteristics and patterns. Because propaganda usually comes to us unlabeled and unannounced, identifying the different categories of propaganda not only provides the propagandist more options for persuasion, but brings to light often hidden forms of propaganda to the critic. The categories come in binary pairs: 1) vertical/horizontal; 2) political/sociological; 3) covert/covert; 4) agitation/integration; 5) rational/irrational. Importantly, one from each pair can be combined to produce new forms of expression, as for instance vertical and political and irrational would produce a polemical rant by a self-identified ideologue, while covert and sociological and horizontal would anonymously try to introduce new forms of expression in casual conversation to influence youth trends. Let us take each pair in order.

Covert/Overt

The most important decision in any propaganda is whether or not to claim ownership of the message. **Overt propaganda** accurately identifies the author and is explicit about the aims and intentions of the propagandist. In political propaganda, this takes the form of a candidate saying "I approve this message." **Covert propaganda**, in contradistinction, hides the author either by making the message anonymous or by attributing it to a different, usually more recognizable, sender. There are two paths to delivering covert propaganda. The first, called the **deflection source model**, has the propagandist give information to a public source who then disseminates it without attribution, as when a negative political campaign feeds a smear to the press but denies doing so. For instance, Russian government hackers gained access to U.S. presidential candidate Hillary Clinton's emails and forwarded them to Wikileaks to publish without ever claiming responsibility.[4] The second, the **legitimating source model**, also gives anonymous information to a public source, but then the propagandist actively cites that source as proof of the legitimacy of their message. Thus any information, once published in the press as "news," can be used to justify the propagandist's argument by allowing them to publicly cite "independent" proof of their claims, even though that proof derived from the propagandist. In the lead-up to the 2003 Iraq War, for instance, officials working with Vice-President Dick Cheney leaked information to *The New York Times* that appeared to validate the administration's claims that Iraq was developing weapons of mass destruction, only to have Cheney later appear on the news citing that same information to make his case.[5]

Vertical/Horizontal

The difference between vertical and horizontal propaganda is entirely determined by one's choice of medium. **Vertical propaganda** is top-down propaganda delivered by a single source, usually through a mass medium, to be consumed simultaneously by a large audience. It is also a one-way medium, with the audience being positioned as passive and the one speaking being active. This form of propaganda allows for a great deal of information to be communicated at once in a way that also bolsters the authority of the speaker while creating solidarity and a sense of loyalty within the audience. Political rallies are vertical, but so too are musical concerts, radio addresses, television specials, news broadcasts, and commercials. In 2024, for instance, India's Ministry of Health and Family Welfare launched the "When You Quit" anti-smoking campaign on national radio stations and on digital television platforms in 17 pan-Indian languages to reach the widest population possible.[6] **Horizontal propaganda** is dialogical and nonhierarchical, relying on conversation and turn-taking, question and answer, community and engagement. Being "horizontal" implies being on a flat plane, side-by-side. Each participant is active and has an opportunity to speak. What makes it propaganda, however, is that this conversation is nonetheless subtly "guided" toward a goal, usually by discussion leaders who suggest the topics to be discussed and indicate the "right" answers. Religious discussions often take this form, as do online forms of discussion in chat forums that often are formed to promote a particular perspective. Horizontal propaganda is slower and communicates far less information, but it often creates more dedicated commitment and a feeling of belonging. Alcoholics Anonymous, for instance, bases almost its entire therapy on group sessions in which "sharing" is the essential communication component, with all of its members committed toward a common goal and yet each of them interested in expressing his or her own unique personal experience that makes them feel validated as individuals.[7]

Political/Sociological

Directness and breadth can be said to distinguish political from sociological propaganda. **Political propaganda** is produced by a distinct group with clear identity and interests who advocate for specific ideas, actions, and policies. This is the form of propaganda most readily characterized as propaganda, taking the form of campaign platforms, corporate advertising, lobbying groups, social activism, or charitable fundraising. Political propaganda has the advantage of being able to appeal to loyalty and identity while providing clear guidelines for actions to attain a goal. For instance, in Northern Ireland, a group known as the Ulster Defence Association (UDA) was founded in 1971 to coordinate the efforts of local Protestant vigilante groups in the province to resist any attempt to sever the union with Great Britain, often taking credit for murdering prominent Irish Catholic leaders and members of the Irish Republican Army (IRA).[8] But political propaganda often implicitly relies on the resources created by **sociological propaganda**, which is a more diffuse, long-term effort to alter general attitudes and norms through the medium of cultural and social institutions, leisure activities, consumption practices, and habits. Unlike political propaganda, sociological propaganda has no clear "author" (even when it does, that author has no political program) and its message advocates no particular action. Rather, through movies, music, architecture, art, literature, sports, sitcoms, plays, hobbies, or holidays, sociological propaganda slowly constructs a "way of life" that simply normalizes collective ways of doing things. For instance much post-World War II popular entertainment created an image of the white middle-class family with a working father, stay-at-home mother, and two children that solidified the norm of the nuclear family even when it did not actually reflect the majority of people's actual lives. But once established, sociological propaganda can provide resources for political propaganda by allowing it to cite those "ways of life" as evidence for how things are and should remain. In the case of Northern Ireland, for instance, even as the violence of the "Troubles" has subsided in recent decades, there remains vibrant celebrations (including giant bonfires) on July 12 to celebrate the defeat of Catholic armies led by King James II by the Protestant forces of William of Orange. Although criticized for instigating sectarian violence, leaders of the political establishment deny such connection, one arguing that "It is about publicly expressing our faith, our culture, our heritage. It is about celebrating, respectfully, our identity."[9] This is the very definition of the function of sociological propaganda.

Agitation/Integration

These two forms of propaganda are determined by the relationship between the audience and some institutional or governmental authority. **Agitation propaganda** seeks to arouse hatred, contempt, resentment, and indignation against authority by showing it to be fundamentally abusive and unjust. Strategies of pathos are clearly central to agitation propaganda, with exaggeration, conspiracy theory, violence, polarization, and urgency being some of its dominant characteristics. This desired outcome is usually to separate its audience from their social group and liberate them for extreme action. Certainly this is the propaganda of terrorism and war, but it is also characteristic of political propaganda at the extremes, attractive in part because it provides a heroic persona that flatters its hearers and makes their lives extraordinary. Integration propaganda is then what happens "after the war." **Integration propaganda** seeks to reconcile the audience with authority by finding a place for the individual within the social structure. Quite literally this is what the task of various veterans' groups perform, especially after traumatic experiences of conflict and disruption. Integration propaganda provides a more fraternal or maternal image of authority as a caring parent who wishes to bring a family together again. What is crucial to its success, however, is not just the image of integration but the actual practice of giving people something positive to do. Integration propaganda largely succeeds because it expends resources and actually follows through on his promises by providing jobs, resources, and a place to feel at home. Integration heals the scars caused by agitation through collective practice.

Rational/Irrational

The final propaganda pair determines the relationship between the message and the facts. Too often, people assume that propaganda must be constituted by lies if it is to be propaganda. This is not the case. It has long been known by professional propagandists, the Nazi Joseph Goebbels being the most notorious, that the most effective propaganda makes use of accepted and even incontrovertible facts even as it draws the wildest conclusions from them. **Rational**

propaganda represents this effort to drown its audience and facts in order to build out of this chaos a vague but powerful mythic conclusion. Unlike scientific or legal argumentation, which stays very close to evidence and works methodologically, step-by-step, to a conclusion, rational propaganda often plays loose with the facts. Examine any particular fact in this propaganda and one might be convinced that it is valid. And some propaganda may, in fact, be reliable. But for much so-called "rational" propaganda, you step back and suddenly the facts blur into some unverifiable myth. This is the preferred propaganda of conspiracy theorists and political polemicists. One of the most widespread phenomena is the QAnon conspiracy theory, which works by leaving "crumbs" of evidence for followers to pick up and "bake" into a conclusion, usually revealing some secret cabal of pedophiles and Satan-worshipers.[10] Rational propaganda thus claims to be based in facts, but much of it only provides the illusion of evidence to validate some preestablished prejudice. **Irrational propaganda** by contrast has no patience for puzzles and facts. It goes right to the heart of myth and draws the wildest caricatures of good and evil to demonize the opponent and put the audience on the side of the angels. Because there is no pretense to objectivity or accuracy, irrational propaganda wallows in exaggerations for purely emotional pleasure. Slogans, name-calling, hero worship, demonization, cartoon, caricature—everything simple and shocking can be used to its advantage. One immediately calls the mind, for instance, the worst of World War II propaganda posters that inflamed hatred against the perceived enemy, often portraying them as vicious animals in contrast with the saintly, heroic warriors of one's own side. Irrational propaganda is often controversial but it endures because it offers a simple emotional appeal that arouses feelings of pride, laughter, hatred, competitiveness, gregariousness, resentment, and love that taps into a deep well of human instincts. For instance, online chatrooms by self-identified "incels" (involuntary celibate men) rely on simplistic caricatures that divide men and women into "Chads" and "Stacys," which is to say stereotypes of sexually successful men and the sexually available women that sleep with them. Although these have little basis in reality, the irrational images provide a kind of explanation for their sense of rejection and a type of community based on what the men perceive to be their shared condition of victimage.[11]

MAKING NEWS

Although "the news media" is ever a site of controversy, crisis, and political debate, there is nothing complicated or mysterious about the nature of news. **News** is information about what is new, and it grows out of a very basic human desire to know what is going on. News is intrinsic to our being as symbol-using animals with innate drives to construct an image of the world outside of our direct experience. This insatiable curiosity for news is rooted in our survival instinct. One might imagine early uses of fire, smoke, and sound to indicate the presence of food or the approach of an enemy. That use of the news remains vital in helping populations avoid disasters and seek out new resources. But news also grows out of our social instinct to hear about the goings-on of other people, often in the form of rumor and gossip. But even this has a survival function, as such news allows us to diagram in our imaginations the complexities of our social environment and thus help us navigate an always-changing terrain. Today it isn't so different. Anything we wish to hear about in conversation will inevitably find its way into the news one way or the other. News exists because people crave the news.

But in propaganda we must consider news from an industry perspective, as it is "the" news that usually matters—which is to say the news produced and disseminated by mass media outlets. From this perspective, the **news media** is an industry that produces, dramatizes, and disseminates new information that is designed to capture the attention of the buying public. Walter Lippmann famously described the function of news as a searchlight that breathlessly scans the darkness, bringing one thing into focus and moving others into shadow. Because news is always about the new, the news is by its nature discontinuous; it constantly jumps from one thing to another. And what it focuses on is information, which in the news tends to be something discrete, eventful, localized, and factual. Information takes "headline" forms of expression as in "man bites dog" or "war breaks out" or "celebrity gets divorce" or "new technology breaks boundaries" or "debutantes light up cigarettes." News is thus always dramatized into some kind of story designed to capture attention. People not only love drama but use narrative to make sense of complex information. News also frames events so that they take the form of recognizable plots. Finally, news must be disseminated through some form of media that can be consumed and sold to the buying public. News, that is to say, is an industry that must make money. That money comes both from subscriptions and from advertising, both of which rely on maintaining a core audience of viewers, listeners, and readers consuming the company's brand of news. Without the ability to capture and hold onto a buying public, the financial support for any news outlet collapses unless financed by the state.

Yet it is notable that despite differences in audiences, much of the news media tends to cover the same set of breaking stories. There is a reassuring objectivity to this phenomenon. The more that different individuals from different perspectives can share the same experience and point confidently to the same thing, the more objectivity something possesses. By "objectivity" I do not mean necessarily accuracy or truth, as it is commonly used. Objectivity means quite literally that something takes on objective (and not abstract or intangible or hypothetical) form. Despite the long-standing debates about the status of objectivity journalism, objectivity in the sense of being object-oriented is an essential and incontrovertible aspect of journalism. The opposite of objectivity is not subjectivity but ineffability. To be **objective** is to construct a report that references tangible objects, events, people, records, statements, and actions that are open to others to experience independently on their own. Whether a reporter adds his or her own interpretation, spin, or frame to those objects does not necessarily undermine that report's core objectivity as long as that point of view is marked as an opinion. Only when news relies only on intangible or inaccessible data does it lose its objectivity and become hearsay and rumor—the report purely of one's own subject position *on its own*. Consequently, the more that even opposing news outlets agree on the essential objectivity of some event, the more that the consuming public can be assured of its reality, even if they people might differ on its quality or significance. Two parties can disagree about the meaning of an event, but if they agree that some kind of event occurred because there was evidence for its occurrence, then those reports share a core objectivity.

Propaganda predictably exploits the desire for objectivity by creating events that high-spots certain important qualities of things, people, objects, or ideas. **High-spotting** occurs when some event and story dramatize a single, outstanding quality of something that becomes representative of the entire object or enterprise. Bernays, who defined this tactic, gives an example in his campaign to encourage mothers of school-age children to buy Ivory soap. Instead of simply paying for ads showing kids having fun getting clean, Bernays donated bars of soap to local schools to use not for washing hands but for an artistic sculpture contest. The contest was bound to attract media attention because it would feature the creative products of children, all of them clearly future Michelangelos. But it would also high-spot a distinctive feature of Ivory soap, namely its pure white color and texture akin to the marble of Renaissance culture. And as an added benefit, the soap would be associated with children's creativity and play. Notably, none of these associations had anything to do with its cleaning power as soap. But since this function was well-known, Bernays decided to high-spot its aesthetic quality that made it unique among soap brands and guaranteed to catch popular attention. It made for a good human interest story.

What "makes" news thus tends to have universal qualities despite differences in perspective in terms of who reports it. Hence, news tends to be eventful, timely, dramatic, personal, and fragmented:

1. News is **eventful** because it must be an outstanding event that "breaks" into our conscious awareness. Even if some long-standing problem exists, that problem is not news until an event happens that can be captured, recorded, and brought to the vivid attention of the news consumer. For instance, although global warming is an ongoing, planet-wide crisis, coverage tends to follow only in the wake of specific disasters, as when wildfires on the island of Maui, Hawaii burned 2,500 acres because of drought and increased temperatures brought about by climate change.[12]

2. News is **timely** insofar as it must not only be new but also relevant in some way to the contemporary situation, otherwise it is viewed as distant from people's lives and interests. Although homeowners are always concerned about energy costs, for example, there is always a spike in coverage of natural gas prices before the winter season as people are concerned that they must endure the cold to pay the bills.[13]

3. News is **dramatic** because a newsworthy event must contain some element of drama that makes for an engaging story. Such qualities might include being shocking, controversial, unusual, fearful, titillating, mysterious, grotesque, competitive, or romantic. When 33 Chilean miners were trapped a half-mile underground for 69 days in 2010, the news provided continuous coverage of the rescue effort, culminating in their climactic and heroic release.[14]

4. News is **personal** because that dramatic character must in some way feature the actions of key players as antagonists or protagonists, even if there are many other people involved and many other factors at play. During the 2022 World Cup, for instance, the final between Argentina and France was largely reduced to a personal battle between Lionel Messi and Kylian Mbappé, with much of the post-game discussion focused on who was the better player.[15]

5. Finally, all of these characteristics result in the news being inherently **episodic**, insofar as new stories tend to feature events as self-contained stories that are largely disconnected from a larger, more complex narrative explanation. For instance, after a 2015 dam collapse in Brazil flooded nearby towns, rivers, and forests with toxic waste and mud, the story largely disappeared from the news until the mining companies BHP and Vale signed a deal with the Brazilian government to pay nearly $30 billion in compensation. But the news of the deal focused primarily on the deal itself, largely ignoring the complex causes of the collapse and the enduring consequences of the disaster, as indicated by the BBC headline: "Mining giants sign $30bn settlement for 2015 Brazil dam collapse."[16]

It is this insatiable appetite for the news industry for the "new" that makes it such an important medium of propaganda. This assertion should not be interpreted as claiming that all news is propaganda. Such an attitude demonstrates an ignorance of the news industry and denigrates the profession of the journalist. The job of journalists is to define newsworthy events and make them engaging to their buying audience. Any journalist who is not an anonymous troll requires some reputation for diligence and honesty to do their jobs. Consequently, they balance objectivity (understood as the factual documentation of what exists) with the need for **framing** (which is the dramatic story in which these facts are presented). The objectivity is what journalists often share across different competing perspectives, while the political and social divides are often found in framing. Nonetheless, neither of these practices amount to propaganda. What makes news a medium of propaganda is that the events they report or the frames that they use might have been produced or suggested by propagandists. But here's what is important. The news media does not report propaganda *because* it is propaganda; they use propaganda in their reporting because propagandists have given them the material that makes for a good news story. Indeed, sometimes it is the ethical responsibility of the journalist to report on what is clearly propaganda, for the reason that just because something is propaganda does not mean it is not true, relevant, or interesting. In fact, the most effective propaganda is that which can be reported as genuine news.

WHY PROPAGANDA IS ADDICTIVE

Propaganda proliferates because it serves the needs of people in a technological society. Despite popular complaints about propaganda, should it disappear altogether many of us would miss its ability to relieve boredom, direct our attention, and satisfy our pride. But there is a price to be paid for this addiction to propaganda. The more people crave the new and the pleasurable, the more they support industrial-scale propaganda whose goal is simply to profit off of people's addictions. This propaganda of disinformation cloaks itself in the aura of virtue only to peddle vice. If propaganda is ever to serve genuine democratic ends, it must arise within a communicative environment that guarantees not only freedom of speech but equality of access and fair distribution of resources. When economic inequality and the concentration of media ownership results in a flood of single source messaging, the result is the fact of censorship and the simulation of authoritarian regimes of truth. The rise of interactive social media offers some corrective to media concentration, but it has also had the side effect of increasing further the ability to create a bubble of single source messaging and spread viral lies. The inevitable results of such a system is polarization, the stifling of innovation, and the creation of mass neurosis and paranoia.

That said, if we wish to enliven democratic life, propaganda must still be part of the solution because it will never go away.

But it must be a propaganda in which everyone participates as both producer and consumer. To be an active citizen in a modern technological society is to be actively engaged in the diverse propagandas of our time. It means to study the complex interlocking formations of society, to map the interactions of the media ecosystem, to know the necessities placed upon us by technique. It means to consciously promote one's own vision of the world that one believes to be true through methods of persuasion capable of reaching a mass audience. It means collaborating with others to create events that break through the public consciousness and make them aware of news in a way that productively challenges and redirects their habits. Propaganda is the only technique capable of moving, however slowly, the billions of people that inhabit the globe toward a better future. When we seek to influence a mass audience, we should not deceive ourselves that we are doing something other than propaganda. For our fate as a human species in the Anthropocene depends on our ability to act together.

DISCUSSION QUESTIONS

1. Think about an issue that has caused you a great deal of stress lately that did not originate in your direct experience. Take a moment to diagram the situation in your mind as you understand it. What is the nature of the problem as you see it? Do you know the sources of this image in your head? And what do you imagine might happen that concerns you?

2. Was Bernays's "Torches of Freedom" tactic unethical because it operated as covert propaganda? Or was it a perfectly acceptable campaign because all of the participants acted on their own free will, despite being encouraged by Bernays? Define the principle you are using to make this judgment and see if it applies equally to other cases.

EXERCISES

1. The categories of propaganda are not simply helpful in criticism but also in the process of invention. Come up with a local campaign goal that tries to get people to do something unusual. Now select one category of propaganda from each pair and try

to imagine a tactic that combines three or four into one coherent campaign. Then do the same with the opposite pairings. How do the campaigns differ? How does forcing oneself to adopt certain tactics produce creativity? Finally, write a news headline that you believe would cover this campaign in a way that would attract readers while also getting your message across.

2. Choose a popular action movie that dramatizes a heroic resistance against a totalitarian state, such as *The Hunger Games*. Identify the key scenes in which the actors from either side are trying to mobilize mass action and analyze which categories of propaganda they use. Do certain tactics tend to be favored by one or the other side? Which tactics do you feel are realistic and which are exaggerated for the sake of the film?

SUGGESTED READINGS

For a critical analysis of the news and its relationship to propaganda, there remains no better foundational text than Walter Lippmann's *Public Opinion*. However, a more updated, contemporary approach to news can be found in W. Lance Bennett's *News: The Politics of Illusion*, which clearly shows the economic and narrative necessities that constrain news writing.

For sheer pleasure in reading, I recommend an edited collection of George Orwell's writings called *All Art Is Propaganda: Critical Essays*. As indicated by the title, Orwell is particularly insightful in his attention to sociological propaganda, and his essay on Dickens is worth the purchase of the book.

An in-depth case study in how different categories of propaganda take advantage of the news to promote and justify war can be found in John Oddo's *The Discourse of Propaganda: Case Studies from the Persian Gulf War and the War on Terror*. This book offers a cautionary tale about how the abuse of propaganda techniques can undermine democratic ideals.

NOTES

1 Iris Mostegel, "Edward Bernays: The original influencer," *History Today*, February 6, 2019, https://www.historytoday.com/miscellanies/original-influencer.

2   A. Brad Shwartz, "The infamous "War of the Worlds" radio broadcast was a magnificent fluke," *Smithsonian Magazine*, May 6, 2015, https://www.smithsonianmag.com/history/infamous-war-worlds-radio-broadcast-was-magnificent-fluke-180955180/.

3   Mark Lynas, "COVID: Top 10 current conspiracy theories," *Alliance for Science*, https://allianceforscience.org/blog/2020/04/covid-top-10-current-conspiracy-theories/.

4   Ellen Nakashima and Shane Harris, "How the Russians hacked the DNC and passed its emails to WikiLeaks," *The Washington Post*, July 13, 2018, https://www.washingtonpost.com/world/national-security/how-the-russians-hacked-the-dnc-and-passed-its-emails-to-wikileaks/2018/07/13/af19a828-86c3-11e8-8553-a3ce89036c78_story.html.

5   Neil A. Lewis, "Ex-Cheney aide testified leak was ordered, prosecutor says," *The New York Times*, February 10, 2006, https://www.nytimes.com/2006/02/10/politics/excheney-aide-testified-leak-was-ordered-prosecutor-says.html.

6   "India – tobacco control – when you quit," Vital Strategies, https://www.vitalstrategies.org/resources/india-tobacco-control-when-you-quit/#:~:text=The%20campaign%20video%20has%20been,tobacco%2Dfree%20film%20rules%20legislation.

7   Buddy T, "Going to your first 12-step meeting," Very Well Mind, October 12, 2023, https://www.verywellmind.com/what-can-i-expect-at-a-12-step-meeting-63409.

8   "Ulster Defence Association," Brittanica, https://www.britannica.com/topic/Ulster-Defence-Association.

9   Rebecca Black, "Twelfth of July festivities 'about celebration' – DUP leader," *Independent*, July 11, 2024, https://www.the-independent.com/news/uk/gavin-robinson-northern-ireland-dup-ireland-irish-b2578144.html.

10 Mattathias Schwartz, "A trail of 'bread crumbs,' leading conspiracy theorists into the wilderness," *The New York Times*, September 11, 2018, https://www.nytimes.com/2018/09/11/magazine/a-trail-of-bread-crumbs-leading-conspiracy-theorists-into-the-wilderness.html.

11 Jonathan Griffin, "Incels: Inside a dark world of online hate," BBC News, August 13, 2021, https://www.bbc.com/news/blogs-trending-44053828.

12 Una Wilson, "Maui wildfires shed light on environmental justice issues closer to home," Old Gold & Black, September 7, 2023, https://wfuogb.com/20832/environment/maui-wildfires-shed-light-on-environmental-justice-issues-closer-to-home/.

13 Rebecca Leber, "Why Americans will pay higher natural gas prices this winter," Vox, November 24, 2022, https://www.vox.com/policy-and-politics/23462844/natural-gas-us-prices-winter-2022.

14 Maureen Corrigan, "The incredible story of Chilean miners rescued from the 'deep down dark'," NPR, October 29, 2014, https://www.npr.org/2014/10/29/359839104/the-incredible-story-of-chilean-miners-rescued-from-the-deep-down-dark.

15 "World media hail Messi, Mbappé after 'most exciting final' in World Cup history," *France 24*, December 19, 2022, https://www.france24.com/en/sport/20221219-world-media-hail-messi-mbapp%C3%A9-after-most-exciting-final-in-world-cup-history.

16 Ione Wells, "Mining giants sign $30bn settlement for 2015 Brazil dam collapse," BBC News, October 25, 2024, https://www.bbc.com/news/articles/cx2dk8yy4kjo.

4

CRAFTING IDENTITY

In late March, 1770, an incendiary reproduction of an engraving titled "The Bloody Massacre" began circulating throughout the streets of Boston, Massachusetts. The print featured a single image of a line of British soldiers firing into unarmed civilians with lines of damning poetic verse like this one underneath: "With murd'rous Rancour stretch their bloody Hands; Like fierce Barbarians grinning o'er their Prey, Approve the Carnage and enjoy the Day." The print claimed to faithfully represent the events of March 5, 1770, when shots rang out in the city of Boston. The city had long been a hotbed of revolutionary activity in the British colonies. To suppress any uprisings, the British quartered 4,000 soldiers in a city of 15,000 people. But on that March evening, with snow still covering much of the city, crowds of agitators, including laborers, apprentices, and merchant sailors began harassing British soldiers by pelting them with snowballs and rocks. In the midst of this tumult, British soldiers opened fire, killing three men outright and injuring two more mortally. Responding to this violence, silversmith Paul Revere created this print explicitly as a piece of agitation propaganda, consciously distorting events so that instead of the result of a chaotic mob scene, it appears as if the soldiers acted as a kind of firing squad in broad daylight upon what were clearly innocent, well-dressed civilians including women and a dog. But the print would not just condemn the British soldiers; it would also celebrate the victims: "The Patriot's copious tears for each are shed, A glorious Tribute which embalms the Dead." The list of Bostonians who

DOI: 10.4324/9781003607236-4

were killed would, in retrospect, be known as the first casualties of the American Revolutionary War.[1]

For contemporary "Americans" looking back at this event, it is notable that Revere never uses the term "American" to describe the victims. There is a good reason for that—namely, that none of the colonists thought of themselves in that way until after the ratification of the Constitution. During the years leading up to the Revolutionary War, most people still thought of themselves as British subjects resisting tyrannical overreach by the king. So when Revere made his print, he was faced with a dilemma—how does he distinguish the Bostonians being shot from the soldiers doing the shooting? His solution was simple but effective. The soldiers would be called "fierce Barbarians" and those who were shot (as well as those who mourned their deaths) would be called "Patriots." Revere was silent both about the cause of the violence and about the aims of these patriots. The only thing it asserted was that Boston was the site of conflict between Barbarians who were faithless, savage, venal villains and Patriots who were full of sorrow, weeping, and a burgeoning rage for justice. This simple dichotomy, however, was effective in constituting a new revolutionary identity. "The Bloody Massacre" would soon be widely known as "The Boston Massacre" and its power to mobilize violent resistance would make it one of the most successful pieces of agitation propaganda ever created.

Although the ultimate aim of Revere's print was to instigate violent revolution against British control of the colonies, his proximate aim was to craft a new, collective identity for the colonists that would give them a sense of pride, separate them from their enemies, and specify appropriate forms of action. For only by doing so could individuals from wide-ranging experiences and lifestyles find a way to act together based on some perceived commonality. Like all effective political propaganda, Revere's print created labels that marked the "us" who belonged to a group so that "we" might both know ourselves and others enough to act with confidence together. Revere did not bother with too many details. Being a "Patriot" simply meant standing up for oneself and one's country against ruthless aggression. The "us" wore the clothes of the gentry, stood up for their rights, organized together, died together, wept together, and would ultimately fight together. The "Barbarians" wore the livery of the British crown, were cruel and heartless, stood in military lines and fired volleys into crowds of innocent men, women, and dogs. Patriots had the justice of God on their side. The Barbarians would be harshly judged by that same God on their deaths.

This example demonstrates why propaganda wields so much power in modern, mass mediated society. Revere's print was only made possible, after all, because of the advances in the printing press, the rise in literacy, and the ease of distribution. These qualities allowed his print, like all modern propaganda, to quickly and effectively define an identity that a mass of strangers could step into and out of with ease as time and circumstance made appropriate. Propaganda, in short, mobilizes collective action because of its capacity to create enduring images of mass identity. On this point, propaganda has continually proven Aristotle to be correct that *ethos* is the most effective means of persuasion. Of course, propaganda also requires the capacity to simplify ideas (through *logos*) and to arouse the passions (through *pathos*) to round out three of the essential components of any successful propaganda. But nothing lasting can be accomplished without first creating a shared sense of identity. In propaganda, therefore, ethos represents far more than just the credibility of the speaker; it represents the character of the audience. All messages in some way are designed as mirrors that reflect back upon the audience a flattering image of themselves. Audiences therefore do not accept the messages of propaganda because they necessarily trust the credibility of the messenger; they accept those messages that create an identity for the audience that they find appealing and gratifying. The discontented mass of people previously identified as British colonists readily consumed Revere's propaganda because the new identity of being a "Patriot" gave them a sense of pride and a spirit of purpose.

This chapter explores the many ways that propaganda crafts identity for both speaker and audience to generate trust, commitment, and action. Yet words like "trust" and "commitment" must be understood at the level of propaganda—which is to say, at *surface* level. Propaganda produces the kind of trust we might put in a fast food restaurant to satisfy a hunger craving, not the trust one puts in a parent. Propaganda, interested as it is only in the mass, crafts identities for easy consumption and reflexive action. Thus even when it addresses what seems to be identities of great significance, such as one's nation, faith, community, profession, or family, it does so in the most superficial manner, as Revere's print makes readily clear. Yet this does not render propaganda itself superficial. In fact, the very surface nature of propaganda that makes it attractive and easily digestible is precisely what makes it such an effective method of constituting power. Propaganda sends out a string of invitations that require only one RSVP to set in motion a process of integration. One might spend one's life in deep thought about what it means to be a member of some group and produce complex manifestos, philosophies, and constitutions defining and justifying its values. But if it was propaganda that got that person in the door and introduced them to that group, then it has done its job. Power grows out of shared commitment. And for powerful groups formed by mass participation, propaganda is what makes that commitment possible.

IDENTIFICATION

In 1977, a television advertisement debuted that would create one of the most catchy and recognizable "jingles" of the 1980s: "Be a Pepper." Created to promote the unique taste of the beverage Dr. Pepper, the advertisement opens with actor David Naughton drinking from a glass bottle on a park bench surrounded (somewhat strangely) by smiling adolescent children holding their school books. He then turns to the camera and starts a jaunty walk down the street, singing: "I drink Dr. Pepper and I'm proud. I'm part of an original crowd, and if you look around these days, there seems to be a Dr. Pepper craze!" Soon, Naughton breaks out into a more expressive dancing as he winds through the crowd, pointing to people and declaiming: "I'm a Pepper, he's a Pepper, she's a Pepper, we're a Pepper, wouldn't you like to be a Pepper too?" Eventually, the crowd of onlookers begins walking behind him as in a parade, and Naughton completes his appeal to his audience: "If you drink Dr. Pepper, you're a Pepper, too! Be a Pepper: Drink Dr. Pepper!"[2] Eventually, other "Peppers" would include Michael Jackson, the Statler Brothers, Tanya Tucker, the Little River Band, and Popeye the Sailor Man.

By the logic of the final appeal, being welcomed into the class of "Peppers" seemed to be a fairly straightforward process; one had to drink Dr. Pepper. But on closer examination, inclusion wasn't so simple. The deeper question was what *type* of person *drank* Dr. Pepper. At the time, Dr. Pepper, despite being one of the oldest carbonated beverages in the country, lagged behind the major cola brands like Coca Cola and Pepsi. So the jingle tried to play this marginal status to its advantage. As the opening lines argued, people who drink Dr. Pepper are also "part of an original crowd." Later, the company would clarify exactly what this meant:

> A Pepper is a person who loves Dr. Pepper. So a Pepper can be anyone. And any age. Because being a Pepper is really more a state of mind than a counting of years. The only thing about a Pepper that's sure is their absolute craving for originality. Even what they drink must be unique. Peppers aren't weird, strange or oddball. They're positive, self-confident, bold and willing to try something new. Peppers are proud. And Peppers are popular. So wouldn't you like to be a Pepper too?[3]

The list of qualities is not without contradictions. But what is important is that the act of drinking a Dr. Pepper somehow becomes a sign of one's character, a mixture of uniqueness and popularity. Dr. Pepper had found a way to sell a sugary drink by making it a marker of a tribe.

In other words, Dr. Pepper made their drink a sign of an **identity**, which is the set of qualities, beliefs, actions, substances, and appearances that characterize a person or a group. More specifically, identity is the name for what stays reliably the same about a thing across time and circumstance, as indicated by the etymology of the word from the Latin *identitatem* meaning "sameness." For instance, an actor who played a serial killer in a television show does not then have "murderer" as her "identity." Rather, her identity would be an actor who performs many roles. We therefore establish identities by those qualities that recur dependably over time and which we can count on experiencing whenever circumstances allow. Presumably, then, if one took on the identity of a "Pepper," that person would reliably express a desire for originality in a way that was self-confident and popular.

For the propagandists, identity is neither a monadic nor a dyadic phenomenon but a triadic one. If it were *monadic*, identity could be discerned about an individual in isolation, as if one's identity were purely something one could discover by looking "inside" oneself. For propaganda, anything that requires such existential introspection that is inaccessible and disconnected from the outside world is irrelevant. Nor is identity a *dyadic* affair between speaker and audience. Two people in a void have nothing in common. And since the goal of propaganda is to establish that commonality between people, there must be something else to bring them together. Thus identity must be understood as having a *triadic* character that relates two or more people through some third "substance" that unites or divides them. Imagine, for instance, three stick figures on a blank screen. Now give two of them a Dr. Pepper and make them smile. Leave the other empty-handed and make it frown. We now know the identities of these two individuals—they are both "Peppers" and the other is not. These two "Peppers" have achieved identification.

Identification is the symbolic process by which two or more individuals become consubstantial and thereby unified as a group. The relationship between persuasion and identification was first stressed by Kenneth Burke, who borrowed freely from theological language to describe ordinary processes of rhetorical persuasion. For instance, being "consubstantial" in theological discussions means sharing in some common divine substance. In everyday life, however, we achieve consubstantiality, and thereby identification, whenever we perceive that we share some quality, belief, action, background, feeling, or other characteristic with someone else. Identification represents any such symbolic act of transformation whereby two or more people may find commonality despite their differences. Thus the British colonists from Virginia and New York started identifying with people from Massachusetts once they could identify in themselves the quality of being a "Patriot." And when Dr. Pepper drinkers perceive that they found kinship and other Dr. Pepper drinkers, despite being alienated from the world of colas, they could embrace the new identity of being a "Pepper." They achieve consubstantiality through their preference for a particular sugary carbonated beverage.

The rest of the tactics in this chapter will show the many ways that different forms of identification can be used to bind people together with one another and also establish authority and leadership. In Venezuela, for instance, the late President Hugo Chavez had such a charismatic presence that his political followers came to be known as "Chavistas" and his movement was known as "Chavismo," which carried on even after his death.[4] In the United States, every individual born within a certain year gets categorized as part of a "generation" with specific traits that then are applied in marketing strategies by corporations, such as the fact that "Gen Z" prefers personalization and likes brands that stand for social justice.[5] And in Afghanistan, the ruling Taliban often target those who identify as part of the Shi'a religious and ethnic minority of Hazaras for persecution, often using these differences as rationalization for violence.[6] In each of these cases, people are brought together in identification through some third object, event, quality, idea, action, attitude, or feeling. It is on this point of identification that power the act in concert is built, just as it also serves as a marker to set that group off from others and makes them targets for propaganda.

GRANFALLOONS

To emphasize the superficial nature of so many of the identifications promoted through propaganda, theorists Pratkanis and Aronson borrow a clever literary term invented by the novelist Kurt Vonnegut—the granfalloon. The term had appeared in the novel *Cat's Cradle*, a classic of dark humor science fiction that narrates how human civilization came to an end. In the novel, this apocalypse occurred when the military invented a new element called "ice-nine" that made water freeze at room temperature, something the military valued because it made it easier for tanks to drive over mud. But once this element was released, it contaminated all of the water on the planet and thus made it uninhabitable. The real point of the book is to mock the human tendency to form into groups of us versus them based on the most trivial characteristics manageable—a tendency responsible for the development of ice-nine in the first place. But many of the comedic dialogue simply involve strangers bonding over superficial commonalities. One airline passenger from Indiana, for instance, brags of being a "Hoosier" and takes pleasure in calling everyone else "pissants." Vonnegut names these groupings "granfalloons," a neologism that combines the word "grand" and "balloon," implying something large but empty.

A **granfalloon** is a broad, shallow, and easily marked grouping of relative strangers that satisfies the social labels of hierarchy and belonging. The granfalloons created by professional sports teams for instance allows 100,000 strangers to dress in the same color, root for the same team, and experience pride in a comradeship with people that have never met. A granfalloon is *broad* because it must allow for almost anyone to potentially join, it is *shallow* because it selects only the most visible and superficial quality as a condition for membership, it is *easily marked* because that quality must be able to be categorized by labels for easy identification by strangers. But a granfalloon is not merely *any* grouping, as one might be numbered as a member of an airline flight at the gate. Granfalloons entail an emotional commitment to the identity that makes one proud to be a part of it in contrast to one or more groups that are seen as less valuable. For instance, being a member of the flight is purely instrumental. But should all flights be canceled for time, and then you hear that your own flight is the only one departing, suddenly people will talk to one another with an almost giddy enthusiasm at being part of such a special group. One must have both organization and emotional connection to have a granfalloon. That is why qualities that are considered intrinsic connection to a person, such as birthday, astrology sign, place of birth, hair color, ethnicity, gender, and the like are so easily transformed into granfalloons in virtually any culture at any time. Competitive reality shows, for instance, constantly use such granfalloons to group teams together to give them an initial recognizable commonality.

Not surprisingly, granfalloons thrive in the conditions of our mass technological society. In small, local groupings in which people's lives closely interact, granfalloons may be few but deeply felt. But when masses of individuals are thrown together in unfamiliar settings and forced to cross paths with one another, granfalloons proliferate rapidly. That is because they serve cognitive, emotional, and practical functions. Cognitively, granfalloons carve up and make sense of our social environment. In the seeming chaos of mass society, they provide simple categories that tell us, rightly or wrongly, who is where and why. Think of a tourist map of the big city, with each neighborhood color-coded and identified by granfalloons that serve to help us navigate and tell us where we belong, as in the city of Siena, Italy, in which each neighborhood in the city literally has its own flag. Emotionally, this sense of belonging accompanies a sense of pride, as people might profess pride in being from one of those neighborhoods, no matter its level of wealth or privilege. And practically, it tells us where we might go and how to behave in those places, especially if we belong to that granfalloon and have a sense of being welcomed there. Even after growing up and leaving one's neighborhood to have a career elsewhere, there remains a nostalgia in returning "home" and reconnecting with one's "roots"—even if everyone we once knew in that place is gone. For some granfalloons never die.

An effective granfalloon generally has the following qualities. First, it targets an audience of individuals who are disconnected from their intimate social groups yet also immersed in some sphere of mass culture, like groups of coworkers out to lunch, shoppers at a supermarket, fans at a stadium, dancers at a club, or commuters in traffic. Second, it associates the audience with some tangible aspect of this environment that in turn reflects something about themselves, such as the purchase of a type of drink, a preferred dating app, a favorite sports team or player, a style of music or brand of clothes, or a make of automobile. Third, it captures this relationship in a word, phrase, icon, gesture, or sound that is catchy, vivid, easily reproducible, and recognizable, like religious icons, team mascots, university colors, or fraternity letters. Fourth, it should establish a relationship to a practical attitude or action that makes those who belong to this revolution feel obliged to exhibit or perform, just as one belonging to a religious faith has specific rituals one must participate in to be a part of that group. Lastly, the granfalloon should imply a sense of pride and significance to the granfalloon that makes its members feel, in some way, superior to others, from the pride in honoring the right God to the satisfaction in rooting for the winning team.

To see the power of granfalloons in action, these are some recent events that showcased how a simple form of identification could produce immediate results. In 2015, Dutch fans of the football team Feyenoord descended on Rome, Italy, to watch a game, but ended up instead engaging in two days of unruly behavior, using their group identity to justify vandalizing property, intimidating shopkeepers, urinating against apartment doors, and jumping on cars. The Italian premier labeled them as "barbarians" and had them escorted out of the country.[7] In 2023, the audience of 144,000 "Swifties" attending a Seattle concert by singer Taylor Swift registered what was equivalent to a 2.3 magnitude earthquake (called by one geology professor a "seismic Swift") when listening to the songs "Blank Space" and

"Shake It Off."[8] Lastly, there is a cliché that "Everyone's Irish on St. Patrick's Day." Every March 17, people across the globe celebrate the holiday, with the admission to being "Irish" largely consisting of drinking Guinness and varieties of green beer, quite irrespective of one's actual Irish ancestry.[9]

Although it is easy to ridicule granfalloons for their triviality and vacuity, they are essential components of almost all successful propaganda campaigns while also performing important social functions. Granfalloons are connectors. They serve as a medium through which strangers come together and are given something in common, even if it is no more than wearing a certain colored sticker. They also relate people to their environment by tying them to specific objects, actions, events. And, finally, granfalloons are adaptable. Not only do they change quality to adapt to circumstances, but they often mature into richer and more complex forms of association. For it is in human nature to take any opportunity that presents itself to form deeper relationships when the desire is there. That is why people join clubs and attend reunions and maintain social media networks. Granfalloons may be superficial, but it is that very superficiality that makes them so effective at bringing strangers together and allowing the possibility for future intimacy and fraternity. Modern society becomes richer and more multilayered when more granfalloons proliferate, not the opposite.

AUTHORITY

After President Joseph Biden took office in 2021, he embarked on a more aggressive campaign than his predecessor to convince young people to get the new COVID-19 vaccine. At the time, fewer than half of all Americans aged 18 to 39 were fully vaccinated, much lower than the two-thirds of those over 50. To reach this demographic, the White House convened a series of Zoom meetings with popular online influencers to use their platforms to promote vaccination. By the summer, the White House had enlisted more than 50 Twitch streamers, YouTubers, and TikTokers to spread the message. For instance, many influencers would post a selfie showing their arm after they got injected, accompanied by cheerful graphics and encouragement. Ashley Cummins, for instance, a fashion and style influencer in Boulder, Colorado, posted, "I joined the Pfizer club," while holding her vaccine card, adding a mask and applause emojis.[10] As White House Press Secretary Jen Psacki explained, the goal was to "meet people where they are," and "where they are" is on "Instagram and TikTok with Millennial mom influencers and Gen Z influencers."[11] Instead of creating an expensive campaign to directly target young people through television advertisements, it simply asked influencers already with huge audiences to do it for free.

The enlistment of young social influencers to spread a message to their loyal followers was a paradigmatic example of the use of authority in propaganda. **Authority** represents the possession of credibility with an audience to the strong degree that one's assertions and conclusions are accepted with relatively unquestioned loyalty and trust. Of course, no authority is absolute. Pure authority of this type is almost impossible to achieve, as people naturally question any suggestion or command to some degree. But one can think of the authority of a loving parent of a child, the authority of a trusted therapist over a patient, the authority of an engineer over the design of an engine, the authority of a geologist in determining where to drill for oil, the authority of the Italian fashion designer over new clothes designs, the authority of a travel influencer over her tourist followers, the authority of a leading brand of toothpaste over the best care of dental hygiene, or the authority of a political think tank over the design of a party platform. In short, when we have no better resource at hand to make judgments and trust the source of our message, we follow authority almost every time—and rightfully so.

To appreciate the centrality that the appeal to authority has in propaganda, one must put aside derogatory and simplistic notions that the effectiveness in propaganda derives from the fact that certain people simply want to be led and told what to do. No propaganda can ever be understood by the bigoted categorizations that credit propaganda success to the deficiencies of a certain class of person who is particularly gullible, insecure, and in need of tutelage. In fact, the presence of such an explanation almost certainly indicates that the one making the accusation is the one being propagandized. For such anti-propaganda propaganda is the hallmark of a propaganda designed to flatter its audience and further polarize the us versus them mentality. The fact remains that every adherent to one's preferred propaganda thinks of themselves as rational, moral, individual, and critical. Even when a single leader propounds a message to a loyal group, that leader will almost certainly praise every member of that group for their independence. It is not unusual to have the supporters of the most authoritarian systems claiming to be the true bearers of free thought, individualism, and freedom.

The reason there is so much confusion about authority is that we often fail to distinguish the nature of persuasive authority from the forms of institutional authority that most commonly come to mind. We encounter **institutional authority** in the form of individuals with titles who function within an established hierarchy and are charged with making and enforcing decisions. Bosses, police officers, teachers, priests, office managers, governors, and the like are common representatives of institutional authority. And very often we associate the workings of such authority as command and obedience enforced by the capacity to give rewards and dole out punishments. Thus, in malfunctioning organizations, one might think of the appeal to authority akin to the phrase "because I said so" backed with force—the very embodiment of unreason. But no institution can exist for long by relying primarily on coercion. It also requires **persuasive authority** which uses symbolic appeals to values, aims, and knowledge to convince people to voluntarily adopt certain practices and adhere to particular rules. For instance, the White House could have agitated for absolute mandates on vaccines that used coercion to pressure individuals to get their shots under threat of penalty, thus relying on institutional authority and coercion. But it was far more efficient, lasting, and democratic to enlist persuasive authorities to convince young people to get vaccinated of their own accord.

Understood in this way, we can actually see that the appeal to authority, far from being irrational, plays an essential part in the development of civilization. Human beings developed complex cultures, technologies, laws, and practices precisely because they are capable of identifying and following authority. This claim is not some covert justification for authoritarianism for the reason that authoritarianism is precisely the form of government that lacks authority. The purest form of political authority is democracy, just as the purest form of authority in knowledge is science. The appeal to authority plays an important role in the development of civilization for a very important reason—the accumulation and distribution of knowledge. The limitation of evolution in the animal world is that every adaptation must be hardwired into biological inheritance. Human beings, as symbol-using animals, have the advantage of being able to store experience in language and hand it on to others. The storehouse of knowledge provides the next generation with the advantage of not having to live through (and suffer) the experiences that produced that knowledge in the first place. They take on trust that certain facts of the case are true and that certain practices are beneficial. Thus by the time children reach adolescence they have internalized knowledge that took millennia to acquire—and they do so without much strenuous effort. The appeal to authority makes this inheritance possible. By persuading others to trust authority, and by being able to be so persuaded, populations without access to direct experience or ability to acquire empirical or practical knowledge on their own are able to possess all of it by following credible authority. And when problems arise, these authorities are often the ones to provide answers.

Propaganda takes advantage of the need for leadership and guidance by routing his message through established authorities. If every propaganda campaign had to create authorities out of nothing and then appeal directly to every individual in the target audience, propaganda campaigns would be long, expensive, and ineffective. It is far easier to make use of **opinion leaders**, who are simply persuasive authorities for particular social groups, who then disseminate and translate these messages to their followers. In contemporary social media contexts, this takes the form of brand advertisers trying to convince social influencers to promote their products to their subscribers. In the context of public relations, it means influencing doctors, fashion designers, newspaper columnists, political pundits, and product manufacturers who would then influence the public through their own opinions and recommendations. Propaganda that uses opinion leaders and other authorities saves time and money by targeting only a few central players and then relying on pre-established communication networks to spread the message on their own.

Ideally, effective use of authority in propaganda should thus appeal to the collective interests of the propagandist, the authority, and the public audience without duplicity and manipulation. And there is a practical motive for this communication ethic. Developing a long-term relationship between propagandists and authority can function to serve the interests of both parties, and a propagandist to exploit that relationship for short-term gain by feeding half-truths and distortions risks severing this relationship, alienating the audience, and increasing long-term costs. But this logic often does not apply to propagandists who seek only short-term gain by any means. For instance, social influencers like self-described misogynist Andrew Tate thrive by capturing the attention of middle and high school boys by celebrating the "Alpha male" ideal and claiming that men have "authority" over their female partners. Despite being accused of crimes, Tate nonetheless retains his popularity because he symbolizes a kind of masculine power that boys and young men admire.[12] Additionally, the overall effect of social media on young women has largely been found to be negative, as many social influencers use their authority to promote impossible standards of beauty in a way that produces eating disorders, lower self-esteem, and depression in their viewers.[13] Once again, this points to the larger problem of propaganda in a technological society, as algorithms and echo chambers create authorities that are largely impervious to outside criticism even when their advice is harmful. The self-correcting nature of authority that gives it the potential to be a stabilizing and rationalizing force in society can only function in a genuinely open society in which individuals are exposed to competing views. When technology facilitates isolation and denial, this process breaks down and authority becomes absolute and destructive.

AUTHENTIC PERSONALITY

In 2021, the Boston brewery Samuel Adams released a new variety of beer they called "Brewer Patriot Ale." According to the company's website, the beer is an

> ode to the rabble rouser who was instrumental to the start of the American Revolution...Samuel Adams, leader of the Sons of Liberty, whose meetings to fight for life, liberty and the pursuit of happiness, were all held over beers in the back of local taverns.[14]

Samuel Adams was the second cousin of John Adams, the future president of the United States. But he was far less of a statesman and far better a propagandist. It was Samuel Adams who helped create the "Sons of Liberty," who were the "rabble rousers" who instigated the Boston Massacre and were directly responsible for planning and executing the "Boston Tea Party" which dumped British tea into Boston harbor in protest of increased taxes. Samuel Adams was thus perfectly willing to use violence to achieve his political aims. Notably, the new beer variety has an added flavor that harkens back to the history of its namesake: "Brewer Patriot Ale features the Lapsang Souchong tea strain that was thrown overboard during the night of the Boston Tea Party." According to the brew master, Megan Parisi, "incorporating this flavorful ingredient into this brew seemed a natural choice to celebrate the rich and unique history of our location." By marking the beer as "Brewer Patriot Ale" (with of course the likeness of Samuel Adams on the label, holding up a glass), the brewery hopes to attract people who feel the same independent-minded, revolutionary spirit within themselves.

The apparent continuity between Paul Revere's "Bloody Massacre" and Samuel Adams's "Brewer Patriot Ale" can be captured in the propaganda concept of **authentic personality**, which is a unique and striking character that feels to be an expression of a real and permanent substance that is neither superficial nor ephemeral. In this definition, *authentic* refers to that somewhat ineffable quality of being genuine, true, original, reliable, and transparent. To be authentic is to reveal one's pure and unalloyed substance to another person without masking, distorting, or hiding anything. And what is authentic here is *personality*, which refers to a coherent, original, and engaging character that has striking and recognizable characteristics that mark something as different from its surroundings. For instance, we might remark "what a personality!" when we encounter, say, a celebrity performer who always stands out from the crowd and violates social expectations. An authentic personality thus combines both of these elements, making something stand out while also appearing genuine.

Importantly, authentic personality is not restricted to individuals. A group, corporation, nation, political party, team, or advocacy group can have authentic personality, as can brand names, symbols, and objects. Both Samuel Adams (the historical individual) and Samuel Adams (the Boston brewery) can have authentic personality—although the latter is often distinguished by the term **brand personality**, which refers to when a brand of consumer products is personified with character traits. Apple, for instance, as from its inception have been connected with the authentic personality of Steve Jobs and has deliberately cultivated a brand personality that "comes across as profoundly humanist. Its founding ethos was power to the people through technology, and it remains committed to computers in education."[15] Of course, in propaganda the entire concept of authentic personality is paradoxical. We usually think of something "authentic" as that which is explicitly *not* done for a public audience. Authenticity, we assume, is something intimate, personal, and hidden. But in propaganda, an impression of authenticity is created through a series of highly publicized actions and events meant for public consumption, thus reinforcing recognizable habits and qualities. So when something happens that contradicts this brand personality, there is often public blowback for compromising its authenticity. For instance, the food brand Goya had become "synonymous with the Latino-American dream," but when its owner publicly praised President Donald Trump, who had harshly criticized Mexican immigrants, "people posted videos and photos of themselves clearing out their pantries and tossing cans of Goya beans into the trash."[16] Brand personality, once created, has to maintain consistency if it is to create brand loyalty. Otherwise people feel betrayed.

However, because the task of crafting an authentic personality is so complex, the method of its construction must be broken down into separate tactics. Below are listed some of the major ways to craft an aura of authentic personality, including for people or groups whose reputations have been tarnished. The goal of these tactics is not just to create an attractive image of a person, group, product, or idea; it is to create a personality around that image that is distinct and feels reliable, legitimate, genuine, and attractive. For instance, when the Samuel Adams Brewery markets "Brewer Patriot Ale" by boasting how both its historical location and its ingredients shows fidelity to its namesake, it reinforces its connection to the American Revolution and invites those who drink the ale to feel connected to it. Consistently employing tactics for creating authentic personality will guarantee the loyalty that generates authority that can pay dividends in the future.

Glittering Generalities

"Patriots" were killed but "Justice" would be served. These are the two glittering generalities Revere used to turn five deaths into a portrait of heroic martyrdom. First identified by the Institute for Propaganda Analysis established in the wake of World War I, **glittering generalities** are broad value terms that lack any specific denotation yet create a positive or a defining and inspiring but vague ideal. Glittering generalities are usually a specific word or phrase, like "healthy," or "free" or "natural" or "peace" or "success." In the language of Kenneth Burke, these can also be what he calls "God terms," or those terms that sum up the core aims and aspirations of the group. Despite being vague, however, one should not dismiss glittering generalities as merely empty words. These are promises made by packages they establish in the minds of an audience an attractive, blurry, image of the future that will come to be experienced if one accepts the message of the person or object. If a British colonist saw Revere's print and decided to volunteer for a local militia and start fighting the British crown through arms, they would expect "justice" to be served. And of course one should ideally feel patriotic when drinking "Brewer Patriot Ale." Glittering generalities may often have no clear referent, but they must nonetheless live up to their promises in some way. When Disneyland promotes itself as "The Happiest Place on Earth," it never quite defines happiness. But visits nonetheless have high expectations due to this claim, and the company risks scathing reviews if they do not in some way live up to its promises, however vague they might be. [17]

Generosity

Part of the packaging of the Samuel Adams Brewery is the commitment by its founder, Jim Koch, to supporting other local entrepreneurs: "with a passion for supporting entrepreneurs who are in the place he once was in, in 2008 Jim launched a philanthropic program that embodies our pursuit of better called Brewing the American Dream." Citing over $100 million dollars in food and beverage loans, the company's website boasts of the way it has supported over 15,000 entrepreneurs. This campaign seeks to establish goodwill through public acts of **generosity**, which is the voluntary giving of time, resources, and attention to others. Acts of generosity associate one's name with the interests and qualities of something that, ideally, reflects one's own commitments as broadcast by packaging—thus achieving some form of identification. Common forms of generosity are sponsorships, charity, volunteering, scholarships, or donations. Former U.S. president Jimmy Carter, for instance, was often photographed in his work clothes helping build houses for Habitat for Humanity, an image that solidified his post-presidential ethos as a humanitarian.[18] And almost every major college sorority and fraternity associates itself with some cause in order to show its commitment to giving back to the community. Successful acts of generosity should thus maintain consistency of message to be effective. It is not only the act of giving but also the choice of to whom to give that matters. Part of establishing authenticity shows that one is selective, always preferring one set of values and interests over others. Generosity, therefore, is an act of loyalty. For instance, Olajumoke Adenowo had already established herself as "the face of architecture" in Nigeria, but her acts of generosity in founding the Awesome Treasures Foundation, a faith-based non-governmental organization that helps women become transformational leaders, has earned her numerous philanthropic awards and has made her one of the most powerful voices in her country.[19]

Media Events

By sparking a small riot in the streets of Boston, Samuel Adams and the "Sons of Liberty" created the event that Revere would make infamous through the printing press. Working together, they thus produced what is called a **media event**, which is an active happening that is intentionally designed to draw the attention of the news media to be broadcast to the public. Sometimes these are also called pseudo-events, implying they are somehow less than authentic and real, rather than a genuine event which would either occur naturally or be performed for specific practical purposes. In other words, the violence of that night in Boston was not intended to actually scare off the British soldiers. It was designed precisely to instigate an overreaction that would harm the British reputation. At the same time, one should not use the "pseudo" label to diminish their often very real existence and function. For instance, media events are very frequently associated with acts of generosity, as one might imagine a ribbon cutting ceremony for a newly donated wing of the hospital, a highly publicized visit by a politician to the Red Cross shelter after a hurricane, or a solar car design competition sponsored by a major auto company. Even though these events are partially "staged," they each attract publicity to an issue in changing the attitude of the public toward them. Other media events might be announcements, performances, debates, brand openings, protests, boycotts, resignations, fundraisers, parades, rallies, showcases, or competitions. An effective media event, while ultimately being self-serving, should also serve an important need or interest of the public that draws them into it, even if it is out of sheer curiosity or suspense. For instance, when the 2014 Winter Olympics was held in Sochi, Russia, five women and one man representing the Russian punk band Pussy Riot made a public performance of the song "Putin Will Teach You to Love Your Country" meant to condemn the crackdown on free speech and political expression. But instead of attracting fans, they were beaten and pepper sprayed by members of the Cossack militia. The entire event was caught on video and reinforced the reputation of the band members as fierce critics of the Putin regime and bold activists committed to defending feminist, gay rights, anti-corruption, and environmental causes.[20]

Spokespeople

The reputation of Samuel Adams after the war was over had its ups and downs, as rabble-rousers were less welcomed in a post-war environment of integration, particularly after his efforts to reject the Constitution. In 1801, for instance, Thomas Jefferson wrote to Adams, lamenting that "I have felt a great deal for our country in the times we have seen: but individually for no one so much as yourself. When I have been told that you were avoided, insulated, frowned on, I could but ejaculate 'Father, forgive them, for they know not what they do.'" But Jefferson nonetheless came to Adams's defense, bestowing upon him the title of "the patriarch of liberty," which over the years has done much to improve his stature in history.[21] In this capacity, Jefferson was acting as a **spokesperson**, which is any individual who speaks in support of or on behalf of another individual or group for the purposes of bolstering their reputation and credibility. The persuasive force of the spokesperson derives from the fact that we often gauge something's authority and standing by the quantity and quality of one's allies. Think of calling character witnesses to the stand in a court trial. The more that people who are highly respected by the community take the stand in one's defense, the more a jury will be disposed to give the defendant the benefit of the doubt. The same principle applies to the "court of public opinion." Spokespeople might be people directly affiliated with the person or group, people paid to speak on their behalf, like celebrities in commercials, or simply people like Thomas Jefferson who wished to lend their own authority for a person or a cause, like endorsements for politicians or for causes or catchy blurbs published on the back of books. Spokespeople are the simplest and most straightforward way of using appeal to authority to support one's own self-interests by borrowing from preexisting relationships and reputations. For instance, in one of the more unusual examples of the tactic, former NBA star Dennis Rodman acted as de facto spokesperson for North Korean leader Kim Jong Un. To one news reporter, he was quoted as saying 'I think people don't see him as … a friendly guy," but "if you actually talk to him" you see a different side.[22] The North Korean state naturally worked hard to cultivate this relationship to make him a cultural ambassador.

Overhearing

The authenticity of Jefferson's praise of Adams is enhanced because it appeared in a personal letter written directly to Adams. Once it was made public, Jefferson's assertions were thus made to appear as his genuine feelings precisely because they were not intended for public consumption. The "patriarch of liberty" was therefore not seen as just another of Jefferson's clever phrasings made to please his audience, but a sincere recognition of the virtues of Samuel Adams. **Overhearing** is a tactic that conveys what appears to be one's "real opinion" through a private communication that is made to seem inadvertently broadcast to the public. Typical examples of overhearing are hot mics, hidden cameras, declassified documents, forwarded emails, or correspondence captured through freedom of information act. The influence of overhearing is based on the notion (however questionable in practice) that what is said in private is more authentic and unrehearsed than statements made for public consumption.

Sometimes, of course, overhearing can be used to severely damage one's credibility if what is overheard directly contradicts a positive image of one's personality. In this case the propaganda value lies with the critic, who can use overhearing to attack an opponent as duplicitous. But other times, overhearing can repair a damaged reputation. When someone loses credibility or when public statements appear insincere, a raw, personal, and bold statement caught "on tape" can capture public attention, especially when it accords with its use. The best kind of overhearing, therefore, is being caught being exactly the type of person that one wishes to be. For instance, in January, 2024, former New Jersey governor Chris Christie was preparing for the Republican primary debate and was caught on a "hot mic" disparaging his competitors, at one point saying of former South Carolina Gov. Nikki Haley: "She's going to get smoked, and you and I both know it. She's not up to this." The recording reinforced Christie's reputation as a straight-talking political pugilist and was widely covered, leading some people to question whether it had been planned from the start to give him a political edge.[23]

Self-Sacrifice

The primary reason school children today all know the name "Paul Revere" is not because he was the creator of "The Bloody Massacre." It was because he was the subject of an 1860 poem by Henry Wadsworth Longfellow called "Paul Revere's Ride," a rendition in poetic verse of the events of the evening of April 18, 1775, when Revere was given the task of riding to Lexington, Massachusetts, to warn members of the militia that British soldiers were about to march into the countryside to suppress rebellion and arrest none other than Samuel Adams. Longfellow presents Revere's ride in heroic terms: "So through the night rode Paul Revere; / And so through the night went his cry of alarm / To every Middlesex village and farm, / — A cry of defiance and not of fear" and "In the hour of darkness and peril and need, / The people will waken and listen to hear / The hurrying hoof-beats of that steed, And the midnight message of Paul Revere."[24] Longfellow's poem thus glorified Revere's reputation for generations to come by framing his ride as an act of **self-sacrifice**, which is when a person gives up something one genuinely treasures for the sake of benefiting a cause and helping others. The "cause" in this case was that of revolution, but it can take any form, including a value, a person or group, a principle, or some vision of the future. What is crucial to a cause being a cause is that one does not directly profit from it. For instance, one might argue that one has "sacrificed" much in time, energy, resources, friends, or family to become the richest person in the nation. But these are not self-sacrifices, they are necessary conditions to acquiring one's goals. In the movie *Schindler's List*, for instance, a seemingly unethical war profiteer discovers his moral conscience during the Nazi Holocaust and uses his skills as a swindler to save hundreds of Jews from the concentration camps, thus redeeming his character.[25] As this example shows, self-sacrifice is a necessary tactic for redeeming a damaged ethos. Propaganda makes use of self-sacrifice usually by pairing it with a media event of some kind which showcases the sacrifice being made in tangible form. But broadcasting self-sacrifice is a sensitive affair, and too much attention makes it seem inauthentic. Additionally, should some benefit be revealed, the public feels even more manipulated than before, thus making the individual in effect irredeemable. An example of redemption was the case of the whistleblower in the Cambridge Analytica scandal, a data consultant named Christopher Wylie who admitted having designed psychological warfare tools while working for the company. But then, in a moment of conscience, he released information to the press, including receipts, invoices, emails, and legal letters, that showed how the profiles of more than 50 million Facebook users had been harvested for propaganda purposes. As one news article observes: "Going public involves an enormous amount of risk. Wylie is breaking a non-disclosure agreement and risks being sued."[26] This self-sacrifice was able to transform his character from a person exploiting the public to a heroic defender of the public.

Division

Finally, what clearly made "The Bloody Massacre" such a powerful propaganda tool was that it presented the "Patriots" as virtuously sacrificing for a cause while the British soldiers, standing under the sign marked "Butcher's Hall," wanted nothing more than the visceral pleasure of killing innocent people. The young men who were killed would have, in ordinary times, probably be seen as little more than an unruly, criminal mob. But in Revere's hands, they become martyrs for a cause. This exemplifies a tried, true, and frequently abused tactic for creating authentic personality by creating divisions between an in-group and an out-group and then targeting the out-group for abuse. **Division** exploits the natural human impulse to side with one's identified group against the competitor, antagonist, or simply any group not one's own. Granfalloons, of course, also appeal to this impulse, even when groups consist of nothing more than a colored sticker. But generally an authentic personality must develop from a deeper and longer lasting sense of identity than just a granfalloon—hence the enduring impact of patriotic national-ism for creating heroes to defend the nation against some threat. Cynically, division is the explanation for the old cliché "patriotism is the last refuge of a scoundrel." What this means is that when all other paths to gaining respect and credibility have failed, there is always the alternative to pick a fight with an outsider and then play the hero by viciously attacking them. The reason this works is quite simple—when people perceive a threat to their group, they will rally behind people who defend that group and forget, for the moment anyway, past transgressions. When combined with over-hearing and self-sacrifice, division can offer a potent, and often violent, way of consolidating power. Yet not all divisions must be seen as exploitative. There is nothing ignoble in defending one's group or essentially wrong with targeting an out-group for criti-cism when there seems ethical warrant to do so. Certainly, there is no shame in condemning neo-Nazis for spreading hate. But one must nonetheless be careful when employing this tactic, even for a righteous cause, as it tends to take on a logic of its own. In addition, one must recognize that many social media sites are quite liter-ally programmed to increase division. In 2021, it was revealed by Facebook engineers that the algorithm of the social media plat-form actually ranked emotional reaction emojis five times higher than simple "likes," a ranking that in practice tended in particular to promote posts that provoked anger. This meant, according to one article, that the "power of the algorithmic promotion undermined the efforts of Facebook's content moderators and integrity teams, who were fighting an uphill battle against toxic and harmful con-tent."[27] Division is thus not just a tactic of rallying supporters against opponents. It is a bias frequently built-in to the very design of our media platforms.

WHY APPEARANCES MATTER

There is an obvious contradiction at the heart of the concept of "authentic personality" in propaganda—namely that what is authentic has been carefully contrived and what seems to have personality is entirely derivative. Propaganda, being concerned with a mass audience of strangers, neither cares nor has the time to cultivate actual deep relationships of credibility, trust, and sincerity of the type we expect from our close friends and family. Instead, it cobbles together a coherent "personality" from socially recognized parts and then proves "authenticity" by acts of commitment and sacrifice. One might think of this process like a kid's paper doll toy where the child constructs new personalities by attaching different clothes, items, facial features, and accessories. As long as the constructed personality maintains consistency and integrity over time, then the image is often accepted as reality in the public eye. And this reality must constantly be cultivated and maintained through events, actions, and images that establish meaningful relationships of identification with the target audience without contradiction or lapse. Because the moment when even the most elaborately constructed personality faces a crisis of contradiction, that carefully crafted authentic personality can collapse in a wave of scandal. Propaganda must therefore constantly be ready to adapt to unforeseen circumstances to change its message with the times.

Although we like to imagine that we genuinely care for the "reality" behind appearances, the appearances of propaganda are what we must deal with most of the time. Our judgments are very often highly swayed by our feelings of identification with people, groups, objects or events. In every sphere of life, we must make choices based on our perceptions of friends and enemies, of allies and competitors, of intimates and strangers. Even something as simple as a friendly-looking mascot on a box can have an impact on our judgments, even though we know full well they are just cartoons. What matters is the emotional tie we have to those icons and fictional characters that provides just enough pleasure to cause us to buy this box over that one, to vote for this person and not the other, or to sign up for this policy and not the competitor. But despite in many cases seeming incredibly trivial, placing trust in an "authentic personality" created by propaganda is not essentially irrational. Cultivating an appearance of trust, goodwill, wisdom, and credibility is no simple task that requires constant discipline and self-control. Especially in an open propaganda environment in which any flaw is immediately used by a competitor to undermine one's ethos, the ability to create and maintain a positive reputation is no small accomplishment. As argued earlier, personality becomes authority when a name is connected with a specific skill, knowledge, and accomplishment that have been proven over time and tested through experience. For those individuals and groups that have a proven track record of judgment, there is every reason to trust these authorities in important matters, especially when we are buffeted by so many decisions throughout our day. Authority at its worst can promote a form of demagoguery based on lies, artifice, and division. But authority at its best is a form of embodied reason established through experience in history. Propagandists must therefore recognize the lasting impacts of their appeals beyond the immediate practical goal, keeping in mind that our identities always endure beyond the moment.

DISCUSSION QUESTIONS

1. What are your "go to" authorities in your everyday media usage, including both the news as well as social media? What gives them credibility for you? And what subjects do you look to them for guidance? Can you identify any practice you have started or product you have purchased because you have followed the advice of these authorities?

2. Can you think of a form of identification that you consciously rejected after having once accepted it for some period of time? What were the consequences of casting off this identity? Did you make any material changes to your life or alter your communication habits? How did you relate to people in your old group after you made this choice?

EXERCISES

1. Identify a celebrity whose reputation was severely damaged by a scandal but who managed to make a "comeback" by repackaging themselves after many years. What was the nature of the scandal and how did it change their reputation? What, then, were the subsequent tactics used to not only restore their reputation but also give them an authentic personality?

2. Imagine that you have been convicted of a specific crime (which you should identify on your own) but have finally been released from prison. You have decided to run for political office. Craft a propaganda campaign that seeks to rebuild your reputation and even find a way to reinterpret your past crime to your advantage. At what point do you think this crosses an ethical line between a redemption story and disinformation?

SUGGESTED READINGS

The writings of Kenneth Burke are invaluable resources to understanding the nature of identification. The best resource for his writings is the edited collection *On Symbols and Society*, which takes the best excerpts from all of his works. But the posthumous book *The War of Words* also has a very clearly written analysis under the section called "The Devices" that addresses many of the tactics of crafting identity.

Two books by Jason Stanley provide essential insights into the methods of persuasion, *How Propaganda Works* and *How Fascism Works: The Politics of Us and Them*. Although the first book offers excellent guidance on analyzing the fallacious argumentation of propaganda, it is actually the second book on fascism that provides the clearest breakdown of how much propaganda seeks to create divisions and set populations against one another.

For those who want a deep dive into a particular case study, Hannah Arendt's *The Origins of Totalitarianism* offers a fascinating and terrifying account of the rise of the Nazi regime in Germany. Epic in length, Arendt's canonical text shows how Nazi propaganda left no aspect of life untouched. It thus provides a cautionary tale of what happens when propaganda becomes the exclusive instrument of an authoritarian state focused on flattering its audience and demonizing the "Other."

NOTES

1 "Paul Revere's engraving of the Boston Massacre, 1770," *The Gilder Lehrman Institute of American History*, https://www.gilderlehrman.org/history-resources/spotlight-primary-source/paul-reveres-engraving-boston-massacre-1770.

2 "Dr. Pepper - 'Be a Pepper' with David Naughton (Commercial, 1978)," https://www.youtube.com/watch?v=YXQzaD168FA.

3   "Are you a Pepper?" Dr. Pepper Museum, https://drpeppermuseum. com/are-you-a-pepper/.

4   Mariano Castillo, "Venezuela: Will 'Chavismo' survive?" CNN, March 11, 2013, https://www.cnn.com/2013/03/09/world/americas/venezuela-chavismo/index.html.

5   Shep Hyken, "Selling to Gen-Z: This is what they want," *Forbes*, June 30, 2022, https://www.forbes.com/sites/shephyken/2022/06/12/selling-to-gen-z-this-is-what-they-want/.

6   Abubakar Siddique and Mansoor Khosrow, "Afghanistan's Shi'ite minority suffers 'systematic discrimination' under Taliban rule," Radio Free Europe Radio Liberty, July 17, 2023, https://www.rferl.org/a/afghanistan-taliban-shiite-persecution-discrimination/32507042.html.

7   "Dutch football hooligans wreak havoc in Rome," Wanted in Rome, February 19, 2015, https://www.wantedinrome.com/news/dutch-football-hooligans-wreak-havoc-in-rome.html.

8   Jessica Nix, "Swifties set off 2.3 quake in Seattle," *Forbes*, July 28, 2023, https://www.forbes.com/sites/jessicanix/2023/07/28/swifties-set-off-23-quake-in-seattle/.

9   Michel Buttelman, "Everyone's Irish on St. Patrick's Day," *The Signal*, March 13, 2022 https://signalscv.com/2022/03/everyones-irish-on-st-patricks-day/.

10   Taylor Lorenz, "To fight vaccine lies, authorities recruit an 'influencer army',"" *The New York Times*, August 1, 2021, https://www.nytimes.com/2021/08/01/technology/vaccine-lies-influencer-army.html.

11   "Press Briefing by Press Secretary Jen Psaki, August 10, 2021,"The White House, https://www.whitehouse.gov/briefing-room/press-briefings/2021/08/10/press-briefing-by-press-secretary-jen-psaki-august-10-2021/.

12   Madeline Will, "Misogynist Influencer Andrew Tate has captured boys' attention: What teachers need to know," *Education Week*, February 2, 2023, https://www.edweek.org/leadership/misogynist-influencer-andrew-tate-has-captured-boys-attention-what-teachers-need-to-know/2023/02.

13   Kim Elsesser, "Here's how Instagram harms young women according to research," *Forbes*, October 10, 2021, https://www.forbes.com/sites/kimelsesser/2021/10/05/heres-how-instagram-harms-young-women-according-to-research/.

14   "Introducing Brewer Patriot Ale," Sam Adams Boston Taproom, https://www.samadamsbostontaproom.com/blog/2021/introducing-brewer-patriot-ale.

15   Leander Kahney, "Apple: It's all about the brand," Wired, December 4, 2002, https://www.wired.com/2002/12/apple-its-all-about-the-brand/.

16   Farah Stockman, Kate Kelly, and Jennifer Medina, "How buying beans became a political statement," *The New York Times*, July 19, 2020, https://www.nytimes.com/2020/07/19/us/goya-trump-hispanic-vote.html.

17 Calista C., "What the happiest place on earth can teach us about happiness," Medium, August 24, 2022, https://medium.com/illumination/what-the-happiest-place-on-earth-can-teach-us-about-happiness-706ea6c9e9e2.

18 "Jimmy and Rosalynn Carter," Habitat for Humanity, https://www.habitat.org/ap/about/how-we-began/role-of-jimmy-and-rosalynn-carter.

19 Lauren Said-Moorhouse, Florence Obondo, and Marc Hoeferlin, "Olajumoke Adenowo: Nigeria's star architect on how she made it," CNN, January 5, 2015, https://www.cnn.com/2014/12/04/world/africa/olajumoke-adenowo-nigerias-star-architect/index.html.

20 "Russian militia attacks Pussy Riot members in Sochi," CBS News, February 19, 2014, https://www.cbsnews.com/news/pussy-riot-attacked-at-winter-olympics-2014-by-cossacks-in-sochi/.

21 Thomas Jefferson, "From Thomas Jefferson to Samuel Adams, 29 March 1801," Founders Online, https://founders.archives.gov/documents/Jefferson/01-33-02-0421.

22 "Dennis Rodman: 'People don't see … the good side' of North Korea," ABC News, June 23, 2017, https://abcnews.go.com/International/dennis-rodman-people-good-side-north-korea/story?id=48224976.

23 Philip Elliott, "Why some suspect Christie's hot mic moment was no accident," Time, January 11, 2024, https://time.com/6554200/chris-christie-hot-mic-comments/.

24 Henry Wadsworth Longfellow, "Paul Revere's ride," Paul Revere House, https://www.paulreverehouse.org/longfellows-poem/.

25 Olivia B. Waxman, "'He was sent by God to take care of us': Inside the real story behind Schindler's List," Time, December 7, 2018, https://time.com/5470613/schindlers-list-true-story/.

26 Carole Cadwalladr, "'I made Steve Bannon's psychological warfare tool': meet the data war whistleblower," The Guardian, March 18, 2018, https://www.theguardian.com/news/2018/mar/17/data-war-whistleblower-christopher-wylie-faceook-nix-bannon-trump.

27 Jeremy B. Merrill and Will Oremus, "Five points for anger, one for a 'like': How Facebook's formula fostered rage and misinformation," The Washington Post, October 26, 2021, https://www.washingtonpost.com/technology/2021/10/26/facebook-angry-emoji-algorithm/.

5

SIMPLIFYING IDEAS

In 1943, at the height of World War II, the federal government released a poster encouraging US civilians to "join a car-sharing club TODAY!" The goal was not to cut down on traffic or encourage social interaction. It was to reduce the consumption of resources by U.S. civilians. At the time, gasoline supplies were limited due to the enormous need for the war while rubber was also running low due to the fact the Japanese military had cut off access to raw materials needed for its production. Because of these constraints, getting ordinary Americans to conserve these resources would play a small but important part in the war effort. The poster, however, adopted an unusual tactic for promoting carpooling. It showed a well-dressed businessman in a fedora driving his convertible seemingly comfortably to work. But he was not alone. Beside him was a transparent figure, outlined in white, with a German cross on his military jacket and an eerily familiar mustache. At the top of the poster read the warning: "When you ride ALONE you ride with HITLER!" Thus the seemingly oblivious businessman, concerned with his own interests and comforts, was actually assisting Hitler's commute to work, as if the man would be dropping Hitler off at his underground bunker from which he would direct the war against the United States.[1]

Although today the image has become popularized as a piece of retro art designed to provoke laughter, at the time it was making a very serious claim. The poster connected one's daily commute to the use of rubber and gas which was then seen to cause a reduction

DOI: 10.4324/9781003607236-5

in military readiness leading ultimately to the defeat of the US in the war and the enabling of Hitler's totalitarian conquest. It was exaggerated, to be sure, but it was also based on causal facts supported by statistical analysis. The portrayal of Hitler literally riding beside the businessman effectively collapses the entire causal sequence into a single, powerful symbol. Nobody was supposed to take the image *literally*; but they *were* supposed to take it *seriously*. The poster thus accomplished one of the primary aims of propaganda, which is to simplify the complex series of ideas into a single, memorable inference that anyone can understand and then act upon. By accomplishing this task, the poster organized public actions of strangers to join together and share a commute in order to do their part for victory.

The task of simplifying ideas represents the cognitive aspect of propaganda. Whereas crafting identity defines the common substance that holds a group together, simplifying ideas gives them maps, guidelines, and instructions that tells them what exists, why it exists, what to do, and where to go. To simplify ideas is akin to filling in the details of a tourist map to help enthusiastic visitors find their way around a foreign city by constructing piece by piece the mosaic of a pseudo-environment. **Simplifying ideas** thus means the process of making complicated, abstract, or distant matters easy to understand, concrete, and relevant to an audience in a way that stimulates peripheral route processing and provokes reflex actions desired by the propagandist. An idea, as I have said previously, is any act of cognition that connects two or more things and contains some mental conception of the world, whether imaginary or real. And by "simplification" I mean a reduction and representation of even the most complex system or relationship or process to some basic proposition that can be intuitively grasped in an icon or phrase. Importantly, simplification should not be conflated with *over*-simplification, which implies intentional distortion for the purposes of misleading an audience. Simplification on its own has a long-established tradition in education, motivation, translation, and edification. All forms of early literacy in primary schooling rely on simplifications to introduce complex topics to early learners. Scientific theories use simplified formulas and diagrams and thought experiments to communicate abstract ideas. Religions are adept at reducing metaphysical ideas to icons, symbols, pictures, maxims, and rituals. And military strategies would be impossible without simplifications of battlefields, resources, armies, and tactics. Simplification, when done with sensitivity and expertise, identifies the essential relevant qualities of something and puts those things in a form adapted to the beliefs, values, and habits of an audience so that people can access and use these qualities for their own advantage. Simplification becomes **over-simplification** when misleading or even false qualities are made central to the representation in order to manipulate an audience into believing what is clearly untrue or even harmful.

The public debates over climate change, for instance, are inevitably fought using different forms of simplification. The most frequent analogy used in scientific textbooks is the "greenhouse effect," often with images of a literal greenhouse as a form of demonstration. The NASA website even adds a second simplification to help viewers imagine the process: "The greenhouse effect is the process through which heat is trapped near Earth's surface by substances known as 'greenhouse gases.' Imagine these gases as a cozy blanket enveloping our planet, helping to maintain a warmer temperature than it would have otherwise."[2] Climate change skeptics, in contradistinction, rely on over-simplifications that conflate short-term fluctuations in weather with long-term trends in climate. A notable example of this was in January 2019, during an exceptionally cold spell in the United States, when then-President Donald Trump tweeted: "Be careful and try staying in your house. Large parts of the Country are suffering from tremendous amounts of snow and near record setting cold. Amazing how big this system is. Wouldn't be bad to have a little of that good old fashioned Global Warming right now!"[3] Trump relies on the logic that a single outlier disproves a statistical rule, which in effect rejects NASA's scientific reasoning.

This chapter explores the common tactics for simplifying ideas in a way that appeals to peripheral route reprocessing. These tactics also return to the discussion of motives as shorthand for situations. Most simplifications involve constructing a situation in such a way that certain actions seem appropriate, easy, and effective. Simplifications thus usually involve some combination of causal explanation, categorical identification, prediction, comparison, and situational diagnosis. In other words, propaganda seeks to place us in a clearly defined situation in which one action seems superior to all other alternatives. A simplified idea thus acts as a kind of sign-post that tells us "this way!" It makes us feel confident that we are headed in the right direction. The value of simplified ideas is thus determined by whether we reach our destination as well as what we had to sacrifice on the way to our goal.

INFERENTIAL LEAPS

There is something rather remarkable about the appeal of the propaganda poster advocating for carpooling in wartime. The logic of the inference is both simple and outstanding. A businessman gets ready for his day and steps inside of his new car to go to work; but instead of enjoying the fresh breeze in his convertible during his daily commute, he feels guilty and anxious because he feels the tangible, but invisible, presence of someone beside him. It is Adolf Hitler, calmly sitting in the passenger seat in his military dress uniform. One can, of course, explain the larger situational context to this metaphor and map all the ways to cognitively get from one place to another. But it is nonetheless somewhat wondrous that individuals doing ordinary tasks during the day can feel, so viscerally, a connection with a man they have never met in a situation they have never directly encountered. Yet after seeing the poster, commuters experience guilt by comprehending how they have aided and abetted a foreign dictator across the ocean. This is all due to the innate human capacity to make inferences to influence belief and behavior.

We can explain this inferential process by returning to the notion of human beings as symbol-using animals. Like that of all higher mammals, the human mind is an inferential machine for reading the signs of its environment. The primary difference between the humans and other mammals in terms of communication is that humans use symbols whereas animals rely only on signs. A **sign** is an index in the material world that directly indicates the presence of something else, like how the smell of salt air indicates the ocean or the presence of smoke is an index of fire. Signs inhabit the realm of the senses and become ingrained in our bodily habits and reflexes, allowing humans and animals alike to navigate their physical environment, avoiding threats and attaining desired objects. A **symbol**, in contradistinction, has only an arbitrary connection with its object dictated by convention and use. The word "smoke" calls to mind an image of actual smoke even though it is just a collection of letters. Moreover, it may be understood metaphorically to indicate, say, a decisive victory. The realm of signs is grounded, local, and tangible, which is why animals are always so attuned to their immediate environment; but the realm of symbols is infinite and always changing, allowing expansion of possibility and unlimited potential for manipulation and distortion. Even a command given to a dog is not understood as a symbol, but as a verbal sound tied to a specific action that acts as a stimulus and response.

To understand the cognitive appeal of propaganda, one must always keep in mind the centrality of inferential thinking to human judgment. An **inference** is the process by which the mind makes a leap from the known to the unknown. The **known** means both that which we perceive before us and what we take for granted. Sense perceptions are knowns, but so, too, are pre-existing beliefs and ideas. The **unknown** refers more to that which isn't immediately present to our awareness. Something hidden, distant, intangible, or absent represents an unknown. In the case of global warming, for instance, we might "know" that we are experiencing record-breaking cold weather just as we might "know" the theory of global warming. But what is "unknown" might be whether (for climate skeptics) that cold day is proof that global warming doesn't exist or whether (for climate activists) it is proof that global warming is creating extreme weather events. Therefore, when propaganda works to simplify ideas, it creates patterns of inference that smooth the way from a known to an unknown. Think of inference as a pathway between two points. First, propaganda brings to our attention a known by making it salient and more vivid than its competitors. Second, propaganda symbolically clears a path to its desired unknown, pointing in a specific direction and making it easy for an audience to connect the dots. In sum, anything that we perceive, hold, possess, or grasp that leads us to imagine some other state of affairs is an inference.

Clearly, simplifying ideas through direct inferential leaps comes with great benefits and great risks. Mass culture benefits when propaganda provides simple cues, instructions, and connections that help masses of people coordinate activities and develop shared understanding. For instance, after the global outbreak of a highly contagious virus in January 2020, scientists at the World Health Organization (WHO) raced to give it a formal name. Initially dubbed the "Wuhan virus" because of its origin in Wuhan, China, the WHO wanted a name that did not stigmatize a specific region. The name COVID-19 was invented ("COVI" for coronavirus, "D" for disease, and "19" for the year 2019). As one of the scientists involved in the name change remarked, there were persuasive concerns at stake beyond considerations of stigma. "The attempt is to describe a disease using terms that people can understand as well as possible" so as "not to be too jargon-y."[4] The goal was to provide a simple way of diagnosing symptoms that would leap from a known (fever, difficulty breathing, loss of taste) to an unknown (the infection by the COVID-19 virus). But this medical propaganda, designed to facilitate a collective response to a pandemic, was unable to fully overcome the propaganda of disinformation and slander. The label "Wuhan virus" or "China virus" continued to be used in polarizing propaganda, leading to people of Asian descent around the world to be subjected to attacks, threats, racist abuse, and discrimination.[5] Whereas an inferential leap tried to help people seek medical treatment, the other encouraged them to target others for blame. Both tactics relied on the power of inferential leaps to direct mass action. The task is to develop messages that help our inferences be accurate, efficient, and humane.

PACKAGING

Anything brought before the public must be presented in a package. When Paul Revere recast a gang of rabble rousers as a crowd of well-dressed gentry, he packaged them. When the Samuel Adams Brewery included a picture of an affable tavern owner on its beer rather than the militant organizer responsible for provoking a war, it chose a more socially welcoming package. And when the federal government wanted people to reject the idea of driving alone to work, it packaged it by associating it with Hitler. **Packaging** represents an accessible outward presentation of something crafted specifically to be easily recognized and interpreted by a mass audience as satisfying or threatening some interest. Anything can be packaged, not just objects but events, actions, people, and ideas. Packaging by no means establishes authenticity or veracity, but it is nonetheless essential as a precondition for recognition. For instance, violinist Joshua Bell is known as one of the best classical musicians in the world, regularly performing sold-out shows with tickets of $100 apiece. But then he participated in an experiment in which he performed for almost an hour in a New York Subway without packaging himself as "Joshua Bell." Instead of attracting a delighted crowd, he managed to only convince seven out of 1,070 people to pause for a minute and give him a total of $32 in change.[6] Without the package of his reputation, people were not able to identify his performance as potentially satisfying their interests. The music was the same, but no one paid attention to it. Without his name, he had become invisible.

Packaging is therefore like a promise; it tells an audience that when one interacts with this person or thing, certain experiences or qualities will result that will give some kind of satisfaction. It is therefore a set of signs that direct an audience to make inferential leaps. But packages are promises only. They must follow through to prove these claims to be true. Packaging represents the creation of a public-facing identity designed to capture attention, quickly identify the object, and convey how it will satisfy or threaten certain needs. In its most literal sense, the box in which one sells a product is a package. The box is not itself the object of desire; it simply contains the product. But the box (the known) communicates through inference the nature of what is inside (the unknown). A dating app is like a package this way. It presents an appearance, a container as it were, of the actual person who is supposed to show up for the date. The cover of the book is a package, as is the abstract of an article, the front of the café, the flag of the country, the symbol of a faith, the T-shirt of a running race. A package is meant to broadcast what something is without itself purporting to be the object.

Another way to think about packaging is through the concept of heuristics. A **heuristic** is a pragmatic cue for solving an immediate, practical problem. Heuristics are shorthands for judgment, in which the "cue" is an immediately recognizable sign that indicates the criteria to be used to make a choice. Although all spheres of practice rely on heuristics, no matter how specialized, the heuristics used in propaganda must be commonly used and easily recognized by a mass audience. For instance, highly technical laboratory researchers use heuristics to interpret data, just as researchers developed heuristics to determine actual COVID-19 infection rates from specific measures. But these heuristics are too specialized to be useful in propaganda. The packages produced for mass consumption must rely on cues familiar to everyone and applicable in ordinary life, such as the simple heuristic that two solid lines on a COVID-19 test indicate the presence of the virus.[7] Keep in mind that commonly used heuristics solve problems by providing quick ways to size up situations and make appropriate choices, such as whether a positive test means to self-quarantine. A common choice made by tourists, for instance, is where to go out to eat. One article captures some of the heuristics they used to distinguish a good from a bad restaurant. Good signs ("green flags") include being busy on a Monday night, having a small menu, keeping a clean bathroom, and having a wait staff that knows where the food comes from. Bad signs ("red flags") include having a long menu, a restaurant full of English-speaking tourists, and a space designed for maximizing seating rather than for comfort.[8] A restaurant that is aware of these common heuristics can thus package themselves in a way that signals all the "green flags" and marks themselves as worth patronizing.

Packaging uses heuristics by creating appearances out of cues that indicate the ways that what is packaged might solve some problem. Although there is no limit to the type of heuristics one might use, there are many common heuristics people tend to rely upon. The *social proof heuristic* uses signs of popularity and social acceptance as indication of something of recognized value, as when Leni Riefenstahl helped promote Adolf Hitler by filming him being adored by wildly cheering Germans in her film *The Triumph of the Will*.[9] The *price heuristic* indicates that a high price is assigned a better quality and a low price is indicative of something cheap and disposable, as seen in an experiment in which the same wine priced at $10 and $90 received completely opposite rankings depending on the label.[10] The *size heuristic* may have different implications based on context, with home size indicating wealth, a large wholesale box indicating value, or a small town indicating quaintness. The ambition to construct the tallest building in the world, for instance, is because the city that holds such a building is then seen as the center of influence and power, which one critic refers to as "Vanity Height."[11] *Color heuristics* are ubiquitous, with colors like red with danger or hotness or brown being earthy and organic. The European Green Party, for instance, uses the color green because of its immediate association with commitments to environmental sustainability and conservation.[12] There are also heuristics of *place* and *time*, with authenticity of place being paired with either freshness (recent time) or vintage (longer time). For instance, the tourist industry in Scotland relies heavily on visitors who wish to experience drinking aged Scotch whisky at its place of origin.[13] And of course how something is named and described also acts as a heuristic, with glittering generalities like free, organic, natural, healthy, just, powerful, honest, and pure being associated with something to give an aura that is attractive and promises rewarding outcomes. For example, research found that labeling menu options with the label "vegan" actually depressed food sales because it appeared to be packaging a lifestyle, when labeling the same options as "plant-based" increased sales because it focused attention not on the person eating but on the ingredients in the food itself.[14] Packaging thus tries to group together similar heuristics to create an overall picture of the person, product, or idea that an audience believes will serve his or her needs in some way without any negative connotations.

CLICHÉS

One of the most enduring domestic front propaganda posters of World War II shows a young woman dressed in factory overalls looking seriously at the viewer with her bicep flexed in a sharp perpendicular. In bold letters it reads "WE CAN DO IT!"[15] During the same period of time, in the United Kingdom, another iconic poster was designed that placed a British royal insignia against a red background that read "KEEP CALM AND CARRY ON."[16] These two phrases, both produced by Allied countries during the same time of war and both cultural icons reproduced in countless media, nonetheless pointed to very different situations. The first was directed toward a US audience of civilian working-aged women to motivate them to join the war effort by working in the factories and jobs previously reserved for men. The phrase implied a problem (namely a lack of confidence and women's physical abilities to do factory work) and provided a means of overcoming (by asserting the untapped power of women to perform hard manual labor). The second poster was also aimed at a domestic audience, but this time of British civilians who were suffering from regular bombing raids by the German air force. Here, the problem was less the actual devastation of the bombing and more the threat of panic by the civilian population. "Keep Calm" reduced the threat to something almost mundane, while "Carry On" stressed the importance of performing the task at hand and maintaining regular habits. Whereas the first poster disrupted conventional social and gender roles to meet an extraordinary challenge, the second poster suggested that the way to meet great threats is by continuing to do exactly the same thing.

Both of these posters employed clichés for propaganda purposes. A **cliché** is a condensed, catchy phrase that defines the meaning of a range of experiences, establishes the nature of the problem, and indicates in the most general way a preferred solution area. Clichés include proverbs, slogans, catchphrases, talking points, labels, epithets, euphemisms, and chants. Take the enduring cliché used by Nike on its advertisements, "Just Do It."[17] This cliché has stood the test of time because of its directness, simplicity, and positivity. The cliché captures a range of experiences because of its sheer generality; it indicates a situation in which an obstacle or challenge presents itself that an individual clearly is trying to put off or to avoid. The problem it defines, then, is one of motivation, willpower, self-confidence, and uncertainty about the outcome. The solution is simple: "Just Do It." The cliché signals that progress is made by deciding to stop worrying, doubting, and delaying, and instead just take a step forward and make an effort to try. The cliché thus appeals to people at all different skill levels, from professionals and amateurs, all of whom may not at some point want to exert the effort or who might question their abilities. Nike, the athletic wear and equipment company, sells products by equipping people to do the thing that they want to do. It thus does not so much market their products as market the idea of striving to overcome obstacles. This is why the cliché endures.

An effective cliché must also have an intrinsic aesthetic appeal to it, often using rhetorical and poetic techniques of parallelism, antitheses, rhythm, and rhyme. Clichés, like any effective slogan, should be pleasurable and easily recalled. Think of the cliché, often used in environmentalist circles, "Think Globally, Act Locally."[18] Here we have two antitheses, thinking/acting and global/local, paired together in a productive relationship and phrase in rhythmic parallelism. But it also presents an effective simplification of a complex idea. It communicates the notion that environmentally minded actions are done in awareness of a global ecosystem of interlocking parts which have a magnitude well beyond the capacity of any individual to make a big difference. Yet it also states that a citizen can nonetheless make an impact by acting in their local context, knowing that small deeds, when performed by millions of individuals, add up to significant change. This cliché can thus be used to overcome cynicism or apathy by individuals who believe that nothing they do matters, or that they simply do not have enough authority to make a difference. The cliché encourages actions like everyday recycling or conservation and reuse that can make people feel they are doing their part.

By reducing a complex situation to its simplest components, clichés also necessarily deflect from more complex and often undesirable realities. The use of glittering generalities performs deflection by emphasizing only the most positive ideals and values, just as Nike does not ever point to failures, defeats, embarrassments, or injuries that cannot be overcome. But if negatives must be addressed, clichés also have an answer, which is by using euphemisms to soften the impact of necessarily painful or negative ideas. A euphemism does not, like a glittering generality, have us imagine a glorious future. **Euphemisms** are not phrases meant to inspire but to diminish, to make something scary or painful into something mundane so that we can turn our attention to other things. They encourage us to look away from a harsh reality toward something that seems ordinary. The comedian George Carlin famously ridiculed how the military progressively used euphemisms to diminish and deflect from the trauma of war, starting first with the graphic phrase "shell shock" and then moving through "battle fatigue" to "operational exhaustion" to finally "post-traumatic stress disorder."[19]

Propaganda often pairs clichés with packaging so that a receiver gets the image of a situation as having a certain, general quality and is then encouraged by the heuristics of a package to accept it as part of the solution. But to be successful, such pairings must also work to set them apart from competitors. For instance, South African politics in 2024 was dominated by the competition between two parties, the governing African National Congress (ANC) party and the breakaway Umkhonto weSizwe (MK Party) party. What is unusual, however, is that both parties relied on the same types of packaging and clichés. Each party packaged itself with the same colors of national liberation (black, green, and gold) as heuristics to indicate its values, and each party employs the same cliché (the slogan "Mayibuye!") to represent its political ideals. As one journalist explained, when interpreted in the wake of colonial exploitation and "linked to the idea of Africa, the liberation slogan "Mayibuye iAfrika!" (May Africa return! or Come back Africa!) is a potent call for social justice and restoration."[20] The fact that both parties used the same cliché is therefore indicative of its power to define the post-colonial goal of self-determination that motivated both parties, despite their disagreements of the ways to accomplish it. At the same time, the difficulty in distinguishing one party from the other also shows the limitations of this propaganda strategy. If heuristics and clichés cannot help people see the difference between one choice and another, then they cease to function as a tool of judgment and instead fade into the background.

VIVID APPEAL

After the terror attacks on the World Trade Center on September 11, 2001, many Americans feared follow-up attacks on domestic targets. One of the greatest fears was the release of biological and chemical weapons enshrouding civilian areas. News stories emphasize how just a small amount of these materials, seeping through gaps in windows and doors, could cause great amounts of suffering and death.[21] Sometimes new stories would show images of chemical weapons used in foreign war zones, most notably Iraq under Saddam Hussein. For a short time following these stories, many stores reported a run on duct tape and plastic sheeting, with large retail stores actually selling out of those materials. People had become so terrified by the thought of the infiltration of these weapons into their home that they were prepared to seal up their entire house as if it was a quarantine site. The fact that this threat was extremely unlikely and that there were other, more productive ways to protect one's family and security were largely ignored. The vivid image of a chemical agent slipping through a crack to kill one's family was enough to motivate drastic action.

A **vivid appeal** uses a highly detailed, specific, dramatic, and memorable example of some event to stand in for an entire range of experiences in order to provoke an immediate reaction based on that example alone. Unlike a cliché, which is framed as a generality, a vivid appeal is necessarily particular. That is why its focus is a specific event, which is a single happening with a beginning, middle, and end that dramatizes some event of conflict and change. The method of the vivid appeal is first to select only a tiny part of a whole situation, second to deflect from wider diversity or complexity, and third to generalize that particular event and make it representative of the whole. Ironically, then, despite its focus on the vivid particular, the impact of the vivid appeal is usually the production of a generality, often in the form of a stereotype, that treats an entire class of things as if it were all identical to a single case. Vivid appeals often purport to be empirical and factual and yet often leave audiences with confidence in the most general of opinions. Vivid appeals can therefore become problematic when they are used for social or political propaganda, especially when they might lead to unjustified praise of one group and demonization of another based on highly selective examples. In politics, one of the most memorable and notorious vivid appeals was made by the presidential campaign of George H. W. Bush, who created an ad featuring the scowling face of Willie Horton who had raped and murdered a woman while on parole from a Massachusetts prison. The ad was used to condemn the prison policies of rival candidate and Massachusetts Governor Michael Dukakis, using this graphic case to accuse Dukakis of being weak on crime. The fact that Horton was also a Black man also added an undercurrent of racism which led it to be widely condemned. But the vivid appeal was nonetheless effective and is now seen as the turning point in Bush's campaign in a way that showed, quite regretfully, the power of stereotypes to mobilize voters.[22]

The force of the vivid appeal derives from the fact that it often reverses the intended logical process of demonstration. Vivid appeals start with the event and end with a generalization, thus making it a form of induction in which inference moves from individual cases to general conclusions. But this allows vivid appeals to be easily used to draw exaggerated and false conclusions, either because the vivid appeal is itself untrue or because the generalization is unwarranted. For instance, vaccine skepticism in parents is largely produced by a genuine desire to protect their children. Hearing vivid, cherry-picked stories of apparently extreme side effects by vaccines naturally leads them to believe there is significant danger in vaccinating their children, causing them to hesitate or to reject the idea altogether. But even as vivid appeals are responsible for skepticism, Mayo Clinic infectious disease expert Dr. Gregory Poland also suggests they are necessary to overcome this resistance. When he confronts skeptical parents, he shows them photos of babies who were infected by a vaccine-preventable disease and even shows testimonials of parents who lost children as a result from a refusal to immunize: "It's fighting emotion with emotion and it harkens to the fact that—if you're somebody whose decision model is emotional—wisdom resides with me discussing this on the level at which you make decisions."[23] Vivid appeals provoke fear in both cases, and Poland hopes his vivid appeals win out in the end.

Despite their frequent abuse, therefore, vivid appeals nonetheless are an important part of persuasion and can be used to educate and to inspire. Vivid appeals are used in emphasizing the dramatic quality of events and appealing to the human level particulars. Think of the use of dramatic storytelling and historical events or the relating of scientific discoveries through specific stories and facts. Vivid appeals can disrupt people's habits and make them consider actions that are out of the ordinary. As Wharton marketing professor Deborah Small explains, vivid appeals are absolutely essential for any fundraising effort for philanthropic causes:

> The more vivid the story—through narrative or through imagery—the more emotionally arousing. And emotions are what triggers the impetus to help. The more surprising finding is that showing statistics can actually blunt this emotional response by causing people to think in a more calculative, albeit uncaring, manner.[24]

Vivid appeals are thus essential for introducing the idea of the new and for challenging habit and convention. Without vivid appeals, we would revert to our customary practices because nothing would break through our consciousness. We just need to be aware that vivid appeals can also wrench examples out of context and promote disinformation and paranoia.

ANCHORING

In the Campo Dei Fiori in Rome, names for it being a place for selling flowers, there stands an ominous bronze statue of a cloaked monk, hands folded and chained, glowering at Vatican City in the distance.[25] The man is Giordano Bruno, a monk burned at the stake in the year 1600 for heresy. His crime was espousing the idea that the Earth was not the center of the universe, but was instead just one of multiple worlds within multiple universes, an idea that completely decentered human existence and challenged the medieval conception of God. At the time, the Protestant Reformation was in full swing, and the Catholic Church wanted to give a full-throated defense of the traditional idea that the universe, the Sun included, revolved around the Earth in order to show that the Earth that was made by God to be inhabited by his chosen people, human beings. In short, they believed that people needed to have a center point in order to make just and pious judgments. Bruno's ideas, they believed, would make it impossible for anyone to judge anything correctly. Lacking a center, their ideas would spin off into infinity. So they burned him alive. It was not until the 19th century, after Italy gained its independence, that the statue was erected to stand in judgment of the church, which had not supported the revolution. The statue turned Bruno into a champion of Italian unity, thus ironically making this radical freethinker into a nationalist patriot.

The intuitive and enduring notion that the Earth—or any other facet of local geography—is the center of the universe is an apt metaphor for the psychology of anchoring. **Anchoring** represents the notion that people tend to prioritize certain facts, judgments, experiences, and rules that spring to mind first because they are familiar, proximate, or prior. Of course, the term "anchoring" itself is a metaphor, using the notion of a ship's anchor to signify these ideas that keep us centered, grounded, and stable. But following the Bruno example, an anchoring idea is also analogous to our relationship to the Earth itself on a cosmic scale. Since this planet, and all of its familiar features, is literally the only home that we know, it is natural that we should use it to anchor our judgments of the rest of the universe. But Bruno's example also shows how anchoring can be used in propaganda. The decision to build a statue of Bruno and place it at the center of the popular market square was a way of anchoring judgments about the corruption and abuse of the Catholic Church. To encounter this ominous statue first, and to learn the gruesome fate of Bruno, would immediately make a person skeptical of the Church's attitude toward free thought, free speech, and democracy. Not surprisingly, the stories of the suppression of Bruno's ideas, along with his more famous predecessors Copernicus and Galileo, have been used for centuries by anti-Catholic propagandists to place the church on the side of oppression and intolerance.[26]

Anchoring represents any persuasive tactic that exploits the tendency to prioritize information that is temporarily or spatially first, easily understandable, and vividly distinct. "Prioritizing" does not necessarily mean valuing or embracing that information, however. It only means making a point of reference by which other things are judged. In consumer pricing, for instance, it is usually the first product one sees that establishes the standard of evaluation for subsequent products, such as when a used car lot places the most expensive car on display in order to make other cars seem a deal. Other times, however, the effective anchoring is not to create contrast but actually establish priority of importance. More akin to the metaphor of setting the Earth at the center of the universe, anchoring works to establish certain ideas as the solid foundation for future judgments. For instance, many advocacy groups work with consumer brands to certify them as adhering to certain ethical practices that consumers find important. The Fairtrade America label, for instance, is affixed to brands mostly in Central and South America that have allowed a rigorous inspection process to confirm that they have upheld specific social, environmental, and economic standards in the production of products like coffee, bananas, sugar, and chocolate. As they say on their website: "This focus means that when you buy Fairtrade products, you can feel good about your purchase supporting the social justice movement and making a meaningful difference in people's lives."[27] This represents anchoring because it assumes that the people prioritize social justice in their consumer choices, which means in effect that they investigate first whether a business upholds Fairtrade standards before even considering other aspects of the product.

The ubiquitous impact of anchoring is due to the inescapable reliance on peripheral reprocessing to make judgments. But it signals more than that, too. Our need for anchor speaks of the need in human nature to make judgments based on *something*, no matter how irrelevant. Except for self-conscious games of chance or acts of whim, our judgments, to seem rational, must have some kind of reference point, some kind of criteria, some kind of measure. They may not be good or justified measures, to be sure. But people usually prefer a bad measure to no measure at all. Propaganda thus tries to create easily understandable, memorable, visible, and applicable anchors that people can call to mind at a moment's notice to make peripheral route judgments. There are many tactics, therefore, that can be included under the larger category of anchoring. The following propaganda tactics represent different types of anchors commonly used in propaganda.

Card Stacking

Perhaps the most common tactic of anchoring his **card stacking**, which represents the deliberate ordering of facts so that the first piece of data becomes the standard by which subsequent information is judged. Card stacking can take the form of priority in time, priority in space, or both. For instance, a written argument (which in products might include a label, description, or package) may simply place the most important information at the top in the most visible position. Or a product in a supermarket might be placed near the entrance so that it is encountered first. The first set of facts might be positive or negative, but the effects remain the same overall. The purpose of card stacking is to define the category that is the most important to consider when making a judgment. Pharmaceutical ads make use of card stacking when they stress the difficulties faced by people suffering from some condition, often relating how common it is in all the ways it inhibits a happy lifestyle. These facts then make the solution—the drug—seem to be an amazing cure. Then comes a rapidly read list of dangers and side effects at this end of the commercial, deflected by images of happy drug users. For instance, much of the responsibility for the opioid epidemic that began to spread around 2006 was placed on Purdue Pharma that began marketing its opium-based medication OxyContin as an effective pain reliever. Lawyers for over 2,500 cities argued that "Purdue created a market for the use of opioids for a range of common aches and pains by misrepresenting the risks and benefits of its opioids," at one point even boasting that it has created a fentanyl-based tablet that would effervescence in water for faster absorption.[28] The tactic of burying negative information in the "fine print" is a conventional application of card stacking, in which the desire to hear and hold onto "good news" outweighs the rational calculation of costs. But so, too, is the tactic of fear mongering and vivid appeal that exaggerates and emphasizes dangers as having priority while diminishing real and potential benefits of pursuing another choice. Card stacking must prioritize information, but it should be the facts that are most relevant to making a prudent choice.

Question Asking

A more intimate, time-consuming but effective variant of card stacking is **question asking**, which simply uses a dialogic question and answer format to more directly implicate the audience in the process of judgment. This is also a tactic that most explicitly makes use of the concept of the rationalization trap. Recall that the rationalization trap exploits the human impulse to reduce cognitive dissonance and appear consistent and authentic in one's judgments, thus avoiding accusations of hypocrisy, evasiveness, duplicity, or waffling. Question asking goes right to the heart of the rationalization impulse by asking a series of "leading questions" that carefully order questions of first answers establish the premises for subsequent commitments. The idea is to make someone verbally commit to a principle and then ask a follow-up question that would apply that principle and practice (often to the exclusion of some other criteria). Imagine that you want an expensive outfit to impress an interviewer for your dream job, but you must ask your parents for the money. You could just demand outright: "Please buy me this expensive outfit, I need it." Given the natural skepticism of parents for the demand for high-priced items, one might expect the immediate answer to be "no." But now consider the following lead-up questions that might be asked: "Do you think an interviewer would be influenced by the first impression?" or "Should I look my best for this interview?" Or "Do you think it's in my best interest to do anything I can do to get this job?" If parents answer "yes" to any of these questions, they are now in a position to put their money where their mouth is—or they must make a complicated argument for why they are still denying you the money.

Question asking, in effect, encourages people to make statements and commitments that can be used to pressure them into making future judgments. Propaganda makes use of question asking in both horizontal and vertical forms. Horizontal propaganda relies heavily on question asking, especially in personal sales techniques as well as recruiting campaigns and pedagogical discussions. In horizontal propaganda, it is important to balance "leading" people to the right answer with not being overbearing and manipulative. Vertical propaganda merely simulates question asking through asking "rhetorical" questions in print or in speech that are simply assumed to be answered by the audience in a specific way. One of the most enduring questions used in US presidential campaigns was the one posed to voters by Ronald Reagan in 1980 as he challenged incumbent Jimmy Carter: "Are you better off today than you were four years ago?" The question invited voters to make a simple comparison and to vote for Reagan if the answer was "no," effectively ignoring all other factors. The question was so effective that it has been reused constantly by presidential challengers to focus attention on the failures of their opponents.[29]

Decoy

A subtle and creative way to change the anchoring for judgment is by providing an option that actually isn't intended to be taken seriously. A **decoy** is an alternative option tactically created to provide a point of comparison and contrast to make another, similar option appear superior. The point of a decoy, therefore, is not to be a "real" option but rather to highlight the criteria one should use for evaluation. Most people, when they think of decoys, will immediately assume that the decoy is simply a much lesser-quality option, such as placing a 20-year-old rusty car next to a bright shiny new one. But this is not true. In this case, the old car may be much cheaper and fit the needs of the consumer who doesn't care about appearance or long-term use. But now imagine adding a third car which is priced just slightly less than the new car and is placed alongside them both. Perhaps it has high mileage and a broken air-conditioning system, even though it still drives reliably and looks pretty good. Now which of these two options appears more of the "deal"? The new car now seems a greater value, as it is just slightly more expensive than the middle car, yet has none of the drawbacks. The decoy of the middle car has altered the criteria for evaluation, as now it is judged by its performance and appearance in ratio to just a slightly higher price. A good decoy must therefore share key similarities with another option but be visibly inferior in one category. This similarity creates, in the mind, the commonality between the two choices, thus separating them from the other options. Then the mind draws a contrast between these two choices and selects the more superior choice from between them—even if, in doing so, it neglects to seriously consider individual options that might be better alternatives when all criteria are considered. For instance, the practice of offering "super sizes" in products that give you hundreds of more calories for a small increase in price is often sold as a "value" meal, even as it costs more than the smaller alternative. The result of this practice has been to dramatically increase portion sizes over the past five decades, leading to increases in obesity and food waste.[30] Decoys may be used to highlight a better option, but very often they are used precisely to make a worse option appear to be a "value."

Analogy

Although the use of analogy is pervasive in all human communication, they play a unique function in the tactic of anchoring. Often, analogies are used simply to explain and illuminate something significant about an object or issue, as one might think of a parable. But when used as an anchor, the order and direction is reversed. Anchoring with an **analogy** starts with the more familiar image and then judges the subject matter of our concern by that standard. What is important is that the audience encounters the analogy first so that they have in their mind a clear and familiar image with its associated qualities and values. Instead of identifying a quality in an object and then trying to explain it through analogy, an anchoring analogy establishes the distinct quality in the analogy and then uses it as an anchor to look for its presence or absence in the object at issue. For instance, if one is in a supermarket aisle and sees a display shaped like an icy mountain peak, the idea of something cold and crisp will come to mind. Should the display hold silver cans of beer, the consumer will be invited to look specifically for those qualities that were made present in the mind by the analogy. But some analogies are more subtle and built into the language itself. Take, for instance, the term "Third World" to refer to a class of countries. This term originated in the 1950s to classify what representatives of "First World" countries saw as a group of struggling, undeveloped societies that identified neither with capitalism nor communism. But the term also operated as an analogy because it described these countries as if they constituted a "world" that somehow ranked "third" according to some unspoken standard of value. As scholar Avinash Paliwal writes, the analogy of the "The Third World" meant that this world "was there to be won, ideologically moulded and accordingly carved up between rivals inhabiting the 'upper' worlds."[31] As a form of anchoring, it therefore licensed the ambitions of these "upper" world countries to treat them as passive resources to be acquired and manipulated simply by their inclusion in this category.

Factoids

The term "factoid" was invented by the novelist Norman Mailer to describe "a fact which has no existence on earth other than what's appeared in the newspaper and then gets repeated forever after. So people walk around as if it is the blooming lively fact."[32] A **factoid** is thus an unproven and often unverifiable piece of information, usually in the form of rumors and innuendos, popularized because of the addiction of certain elements of the press for scandal and controversy and shock. Today, **fake news** also captures the meaning of a factoid, specifically those new stories that are pure inventions created largely to profit from circulation numbers paid advertising. In the internet age, fake news has become an easy way to make money, and digital technologies and artificial intelligence allow stories to merge together disparate (or completely manufactured) realistic images and videos with plausible sounding text. The stories are then consumed by audiences that eagerly share their biases, willfully ignoring their often ridiculous character because it reaffirms their stereotypes, flatters their pride, and helps make sense of the world in a way that feels familiar. Factoids, of course, do not always act as "anchors," and more often than not simply serve to reaffirm preexisting biases. However, when factoids actually introduce a mass audience person, object, or idea, the content of the factoid often provides the standard for judgment—even if that initial content of the factoid is rejected as a lie. During the 2016 US presidential election, for instance, most of the country was introduced to Washington, DC pizza place Comet Ping Pong, because it was implicated in the conspiracy theory that posited the completely absurd idea that politicians were using it as the center of the pedophilia ring.[33] Even after the rumor was thoroughly debunked, the pizza place remains in the public mind as the location targeted by the QAnon conspiracy theory. Even the claim "this is not the center of the pedophilia ring" still connects the restaurant to the factoid in a negative sense. Even a decade later, the influence of the factoid lives on.

Compliance

Lastly, anchoring can use tactics of **compliance** to encourage people to perform follow-up behaviors based on a feeling of obligation to meet the social expectations of others. These tactics make use of the rationalization trap through tactics that rely on two related norms that regulate our behavior with others: the **norm of commitment** that says we have an obligation to follow through on one's promises and the **norm of reciprocity** that says we should pay someone back for what we perceive to be an act of generosity. There are four specific tactics that make use of these norms. First, the **foot in the door** technique asks people for a very small initial commitment to some idea only to follow up, after a delay, with a more demanding request. Second, **lowballing** exploits the norm of commitment by making a low demand of expenditure of money, resources, or time for some commodity or venture knowing that it will be accepted, only to add more demands to the initial price after a delay. Third, the **door in the face** tactic activates reciprocity when someone makes an initial high demand that is intended to be rejected, followed by a vastly diminished demand that is made to appear as a "sacrifice" that warrants a return favor. Lastly, the **that's not all** technique uses reciprocity as a sales tactic whereby a product or idea is sold at a certain cost or price, before judgment is made, benefits or qualities are added on for "free." This "gift" makes the initial anchor—the original cost—now seem a "deal" by comparison. In each case, therefore, the initial action, promise, cost, or offer functions as an anchor that determines the value of the subsequent request, thus acting incrementally to move people toward compliance. For instance, when Vladimir Putin described the invasion of

Ukraine as a "special military operation," he presented the invasion as a short-term, low-investment campaign that would maximize benefits. But the war instead has dragged on, at each point demanding more and more investment and virtual totalitarian control over the country:

> As the Putin regime approaches full maturity, Russians are expected to pay their dues: with their bodies (under the partial military mobilization), through correct behavior (including denunciations), or with their money—big business is now expected to contribute 5 percent of its surplus profits to a state that is hemorrhaging income while expanding its military expenditure.[34]

This is an example of an initial lowballing paired with a longer-term strategy of commitment. As so often occurs with war, the great promises made at the beginning ring hollow, but people nonetheless are made to suffer for years under the idea that a nation must finish what it started.

WHY DEMOCRACY REQUIRES SIMPLIFICATION

To simplify an idea is to make it streamlined, portable, useful, and clear. Our minds are incredible storage and processing machines, but they are also prone to losing things, mixing them up, and crossing wires. Simplifying ideas allows people to carry those ideas around with them in discrete and lightweight packages that can be quickly identified, retrieved, used, and returned. A simplified idea is like a piece of equipment we take with us in a toolbelt or backpack. These are pieces of equipment we use to navigate our environment, target enemies, identify friends, determine the most efficient routes, warn people away from danger, and prepare for what is to come. Old safety slogans like "stop, drop, and roll" or "stranger danger" or "don't let friends drink and drive" are all simplifications that leave out complicated details, contingencies, and exceptions in order to get to the heart of the situation and detail an appropriate response. During the first spread of the COVID-19 virus, clichés like "pandemic" and "lockdown" and "social distancing" were used to communicate the extraordinary nature of the situation which justified extreme measures of mask wearing and quarantine that would never have occurred in ordinary conditions. Propaganda simplifies ideas so that a mass audience can share a common image of the situation and a clear set of instructions as to what to do. Without propaganda, a collective response to a global pandemic would be impossible—just as it would be impossible to market global brand names, create mass ideological movements, or raise the level of scientific education. Propaganda, at least when created with a sincere aim and when informed by the latest information, creates the conditions for global cooperation.

Today, responsible media outlets must constantly struggle to define the standards of ethical journalism and reporting when faced with the ever-increasing glut of simplified ideas. But in the war of words, even the best fact-checking will never seriously undermine the influence of a vivid idea, a catchy cliché, persuasive decoy, or a headline catching factoid. These propaganda tactics are designed for easy consumption and application that provide amusement, enlightenment, pleasure, and use. The only way to fight these tactics is with better tactics, by developing symbolic equipment that fits better into people's minds and makes them feel more powerful, wiser, more attractive, and more virtuous. There is no paradox to this assertion. In the world of propaganda, our ethics are judged by our collective actions in the degree to which we improve our shared lives. Just as we must constantly expose and condemn manipulation, we should also be conscious of the important role that simplifying ideas plays in democracy.

DISCUSSION QUESTIONS

1. Instead of seeing the tactics of simplifying ideas as playing on weaknesses, consider them instead from an evolutionary perspective, which is to say as biological adaptations that help human beings survive in a competitive environment. How might each of the mental shortcuts that are used as the basis of propaganda appeals actually serve an important survival function when human beings lived in paleolithic times? Do you think these mental shortcuts still serve this function or has modern civilization made them obsolete?

2. When we think about the process of making inferential leaps, the character of "detectives" like Sherlock Holmes or Dana Scully easily come to mind. But we typically think of detectives only appearing to solve extraordinary cases. Think instead about

an ordinary day as a kind of detective work. What "unknowns" are you constantly detecting through the signs that surround you every day? How much of what you think you assume to be "present" is actually based on inference?

EXERCISES

1. Imagine you are selling a highly unusual product of your own invention that is sold on a department store shelf. Define the product and then design a "box" that includes the most striking type of packaging. Then imagine a unique display that sets it apart from other products. Finally imagine you have a product representative standing by this display interacting with customers. What type of interaction will attract people to the product without feeling overly aggressive?

2. Find competing campaign ads made by candidates for political office that focuses more on themselves than their opponents. In what ways do the campaigns package themselves? What questions do they ask? How do they present information? What are their clichés and analogies? Place each analysis side-by-side to determine where, if anywhere, they overlap and where they most diverge. Do you think these packages are accurate representations of them as politicians?

SUGGESTED READINGS

A fine companion book to the study of propaganda is Stuart Hanscomb's *Critical Thinking: The Basics*, 2nd Edition. This book covers many of the common biases in judgment that are exploited in propaganda, but it also provides a corrective by diagraming the structure of argumentation and dialogue that can resist the appeal to logical shortcuts that result in manipulation.

The finest treatment of the use of metaphor in argumentation and cognition remains George Lakoff and Mark Johnson's *Metaphors We Live By*. Offering a deeper dive into the nature of cognition, they show the degree to which all thought relies on argument by analogy. Metaphor is essential to understanding the appeal of propaganda, which often relies on it far more than it does traditional reasoning.

Since this is a book on propaganda, it seems appropriate to use my authority as its author to promote my own work, specifically my textbook *Rhetorical Public Speaking: Social Influence in the Digital Age*, 4th Edition. The art of simplifying ideas draws heavily from the rhetorical tradition, and this textbook follows the classical structure to provide insights into the forms of reasoning, common fallacies, and the usage of common tropes and schemes.

NOTES

1 ""When you ride ALONE you ride with Hitler!" U.S. Government Propaganda Poster, 1943," *Energy History*, https://energyhistory.yale.edu/when-you-ride-alone-you-ride-with-hitler-u-s-government-propaganda-poster-1943/.

2 "What is the greenhouse effect?" *NASA*, https://science.nasa.gov/climate-change/faq/what-is-the-greenhouse-effect/.

3 Drew MacFarlane, "Trump Uses Winter Storm to Mock Climate Change, Confuses Weather and Climate Again," *The Weather Channel*, January 21, 2019, https://weather.com/science/environment/news/2019-01-21-trump-alludes-to-winter-storm-to-mock-climate-change.

4 Brett Dahlberg and Elena Renken, "New Coronavirus Disease Officially Named COVID-19 By The World Health Organization," *NPR*, February 11, 2020, https://www.npr.org/sections/goatsandsoda/2020/02/11/802352351/new-coronavirus-gets-an-official-name-from-the-world-health-organization.

5 "Covid-19 Fueling Anti-Asian Racism and Xenophobia Worldwide," *Human Rights Watch*, May 12, 2020, https://www.hrw.org/news/2020/05/12/covid-19-fueling-anti-asian-racism-and-xenophobia-worldwide.

6 Gene Weingarten, "Pearls Before Breakfast: Can one of the nation's great musicians cut through the fog of a D.C. rush hour? Let's find out," *The Washington Post*, April 8, 2007, https://www.washingtonpost.com/lifestyle/magazine/pearls-before-breakfast-can-one-of-the-nations-great-musicians-cut-through-the-fog-of-a-dc-rush-hour-lets-find-out/2014/09/23/8a6d46da-4331-11e4-b47c-f5889e061e5f_story.html.

7 Christie Wilcox, "What Does a Positive Covid Test Look Like?," *The Scientist*, May 10, 2024, https://www.the-scientist.com/what-does-a-positive-covid-test-look-like-68965.

8 Hannah Loewentheil, "24 Subtle Signs That Often Signal That A Restaurant Is, In Fact, VERY Good," *BuzzFeed*, June 5, 2023, https://www.buzzfeed.com/hannahloewentheil/people-are-sharing-green-flags-in-restaurants-that-signal.

9   "Propaganda at the Movies," *Facing History and Ourselves*, August 2, 2016, https://www.facinghistory.org/resource-library/propaganda-movies.

10 "Wine Study Shows Price Influences Perception," *Caltech*, January 14, 2008, https://www.caltech.edu/about/news/wine-study-shows-price-influences-perception-1374.

11 Jason M. Barr, "Clouds in Your Coffee? Skyscrapers and their Symbolic Heights," *Building the Skyline*, January 20, 2021, https://buildingtheskyline.org/skyscrapers-and-symbolic-height/.

12 James McBride, "How Green-Party Success Is Reshaping Global Politics," *Council on Foreign Relations*, May 5, 2022, https://www.cfr.org/backgrounder/how-green-party-success-reshaping-global-politics.

13 Ellie Forbes, "Scotch Whisky distilleries attract more than 2 million visitors," *Scottish Field*, September 27, 2023, https://www.scottishfield.co.uk/food-and-drink-2/scotch-whisky-distilleries-attract-more-than-2-million-visitors/.

14 Paul Shapiro, "Vegan: The product label which shall not be named," *FoodDive*, Oct. 5, 2023, https://www.fooddive.com/news/vegan-the-product-label-which-shall-not-be-named/695501/.

15 "We Can Do It!" *National Museum of American History*, https://americanhistory.si.edu/collections/nmah_538122.

16 Jacopo Prisco, "Keep calm: The story behind the UK's most famous poster design," *CNN*, November 1, 2017, https://www.cnn.com/style/article/keep-calm-poster/index.html.

17 Manuela López Restrepo, "Just Do It: How the iconic Nike tagline built a career for the late Dan Wieden," *NPR*, October 6, 2022, https://www.npr.org/2022/10/06/1127032721/nike-just-do-it-slogan-success-dan-wieden-kennedy-dies.

18 Paul Bubbosh, "Rethinking "Think Globally, Act Locally,"" *George Mason University*, https://cesp.gmu.edu/rethinking-think-globally-act-locally/.

19 Mark Peters, "George Carlin: Euphemism Fighter Supreme," *McSweeney's*, May 19, 2017, https://www.mcsweeneys.net/articles/george-carlin-euphemism-fighter-supreme.

20 Corinne Sandwith, "Mayibuye! The 100-year-old slogan that's stirred up divisions in South Africa's elections," *The Conversation*, May 27, 2024, https://theconversation.com/mayibuye-the-100-year-old-slogan-thats-stirred-up-divisions-in-south-africas-elections-230985.

21 Nicholas Kulish and Kelly K. SporsStaff, "Bracing for a Terror Attack: First, Pick Up the Duct Tape," *The Wall Street Journal*, February 11, 2003, https://www.wsj.com/articles/SB1044820213906360703.

22 Doug Criss, "This is the 30-year-old Willie Horton ad everybody is talking about today," *CNN*, November 1, 2018, https://www.cnn.com/2018/11/01/politics/willie-horton-ad-1988-explainer-trnd/index.html.

23 Julia Belluz, "Fighting scary vaccine stories with scarier no-vaccine stories," *Macleans*, June 7, 2012, https://macleans.ca/society/health/fighting-scary-vaccine-stories-with-scarier-ones/.

24 Perla Ni, "Why Vivid Storytelling Inspires Giving," *Stanford Social Innovation Review*, February 5, 2008, https://ssir.org/articles/entry/why_vivid_storytelling_inspires_giving.

25 "The Sinister Shadow of Giordano Bruno in Campo de' Fiori," *Through Eternity Tours*, February 17, 2021, https://www.througheternity.com/en/blog/hidden-sights/campo_de_fiori_sinister_shadow_bruno.html.

26 Robert P. Lockwood, "Giordano Bruno: How Fact Becomes Anti-Catholic Fiction," *Catholic Answers*, November 1, 2009, https://www.catholic.com/magazine/print-edition/how-fact-becomes-anti-catholic-fiction.

27 "Your guide to Fairtrade labeling," *Fair Trade America*, April 19, 2021, https://www.fairtradeamerica.org/news-insights/your-guide-to-fairtrade-labeling/.

28 Sari Horwitz, Scott Higham, Dalton Bennett and Meryl Kornfield, "The Opioid Files: Inside the opioid industry's marketing machine," *The Washington Post*, December 6, 2019, https://www.washingtonpost.com/graphics/2019/investigations/opioid-marketing/.

29 "Are You Better Off Than You Were 4 Years Ago?" *WBUR*, September 11, 2012, https://www.wbur.org/cognoscenti/2012/09/11/better-off-2012-elaine-kamarck.

30 Dana Gunders, "Super size, super waste: What whopping portions do to the planet," *Grist*, October 15, 2012, https://grist.org/food/super-size-super-waste/.

31 "Does the Concept of the Third World have any Historical Value?" *History Today*, April 4, 2023, https://www.historytoday.com/archive/head-head/does-concept-third-world-have-any-historical-value.

32 "Etymology of 'Factoid'," *Irregardless Magazine*, August 17, 2019, https://www.irregardlessmagazine.com/articles/etymology-of-factoid/.

33 "The saga of 'Pizzagate': The fake story that shows how conspiracy theories spread," *BBC*, December 2, 2016, https://www.bbc.com/news/blogs-trending-38156985.

34 Andrei Kolesnikov, "How Putin's "Special Military Operation" Became a People's War," *Carnegie Politika*, April 10, 2023, https://carnegieendowment.org/russia-eurasia/politika/2023/03/how-putins-special-military-operation-became-a-peoples-war?lang=en.

6

AROUSING PASSIONS

In the fall and winter of 1983, several retail stores in the United States suffered the effects of violent outbursts that came to be known as the Cabbage Patch Riots. Despite the name, these riots had nothing to do with food, vegetables, or farms. They were sparked by desperate parents in search of the latest fad toy for their kids for Christmas, soft life-size dolls known as Cabbage Patch Kids. Invented in 1977 by Georgia artist Xavier Roberts before being sold to Coleco in 1982, the originality of the dolls was found in the fact that each doll was marketed as "unique," as each one came with its own name, birth certificate, and adoption papers. The "kids" were said to have been born in a literal cabbage patch, so that certain promotional events featured nurses in white coats caring for newborns as they were nestled in fake cabbage leaves. As demand quickly overtook supply and Christmas Day grew closer, parents grew desperate for dolls, with many waiting in long lines, traveling hundreds of miles between sold-out stores, paying two or three times their value, and violently shoving other shoppers out of the way to get their hands on a doll. In one famous case, caught on video, a literal riot broke out at a Zayre department store in Wilkes-Barre, Pennsylvania, when a huge crowd of 1000 people swarmed the store for their limited supply of 240 dolls. Images showed boxes of dolls being thrown into the crowd by frightened employees, people fighting over toys, and the store manager standing on top of a checkout counter wielding a baseball bat in the belief that his life was in danger. In the end,

DOI: 10.4324/9781003607236-6

police were dispatched. Five people had to be taken to the hospital, and one woman suffered three broken ribs and a broken leg.[1]

What passions were driving these extraordinary actions? Four dominant emotions come to mind. First, there was clearly the desire of the children for the dolls. But what created this desire? The dolls themselves, while unique, were certainly not remarkable. They had no features that dramatically made them stand out from other dolls. Their uniqueness lay entirely in the framing of the dolls as "kids" that had a birth date and could be "adopted" by children. Something in the notion of taking on a parental role to the doll in an official, legal way (while also engaging in the fantasy of the kids having been born in a cabbage patch) stimulated the desire in children. But the root of the riots lay in the emotional relationship between the parents and the product. Once the dolls became a rare commodity, the normal desire of parents to satisfy their child's wishes became an urgent necessity. Second, parents experienced a rising fear of other shoppers getting there first and making the parent confront the horror of empty shelves and returning home empty-handed. Third, this fear would turn to guilt at having failed to live up to the ideals of being a good and loving parent. Driven by this compulsion, other shoppers were transformed into competitors and eventually enemies, with some shoppers literally tearing toys out of the hands of others. Lastly, these stresses produced anger directed at other shoppers who came to be seen as indirect sources of harm to one's child. This anger gave rise to the violence of shoppers lashing out at other shoppers as if they were defending their families.

This chapter will explore how propaganda uses the four key emotions capable of manipulation by mass messaging—desire, fear, guilt, and anger. Although other emotions, of course, can be used in propaganda, these four are chosen because they represent two pairs of emotions that lie on opposite ends of two spectrums. Desire and fear orient us positively or negatively to objects, people, and events the behavior wants to possess or to repel. One can think of desire and fear as two poles of magnetism, as one might think of a desire of a parent for a Cabbage Patch doll and the fear of another shopper getting there first. Guilt and anger are more complex, and they describe the relationship in triadic terms, with an intervening value principle determining the nature of our relationship with actions, people, objects, or events. Guilt arises because we have somehow failed to live up to an ideal, hence it is a complex emotion in which our pain derives from our relation to a positive image of ourselves. Anger arises because of how something or someone else has performed some perceived injustice or committed some violation. Once again, it is not just fear but a kind of moral judgment. As there are many variations of these emotions, they will be treated here as terms for broad categories of emotion rather than particular ones.

MOOD, AFFECT, EMOTION

The unexpected success of the Cabbage Patch Kids is a paradigmatic case of the triumph of affect to provoke immediate reactions when faced with some stimulus. In the case of the Cabbage Patch Kids, the creative narrative construction of the dolls as children born and adopted by other children somehow transformed a rather ordinary and, to many, even ugly doll into an object of children's desire and parents' obsession. The child wanted to adopt the "kid," to hold it and talk to it, and care for it and be its mom or dad. The parent, meanwhile, responded less to the doll than to the box on the shelf—or to that glorious image of a store stocked with full shelves—and to that same box gift-wrapped under the Christmas tree. The "reflexes" would be the child's immediate embrace of the doll and the parent's readiness to expend whatever time and resources necessary to acquire it. Propaganda did not alter the physical nature of the doll itself but rather the affective relation between consumer and the doll.

When the word "affect" is used in conversation, one might say either that the Cabbage Patch Kid "affected" the child in a certain way or alternately that it "possessed" a certain affect. That is to say, we use affect to describe both the properties of an object or event and its sensory and experiential impact on some human subject. Affect thus tends to situate objects as acting subjects and the human being into the one who "suffers" the impact of the object. This object-oriented grammar is useful in propaganda because it provides a way of centering attention on the things that propaganda is trying to promote, market, attach, or create, rather than on the audience itself. Propaganda can thus be said to "give" something affect, as if it were literally altering the character of the Cabbage

Patch Kid. In reality, of course, the messaging was changing the consumer's perception of the doll, which they then attributed to the doll as if it was an intrinsic part of the product. But it is nonetheless useful to reserve a word for the qualities that an object seems to possess on its own and which seems to strike a mass audience as part of its makeup.

Affect is the dominant quality of an event or object that strikes the viewer during a relatively immediate encounter and provokes some form of impulsive reaction. In this understanding, we should not associate affect with complex emotions that we have for things that we are around or use frequently and which are closely tied up in our lives. Affect relates to how something presents itself to us through sense perception in a specific moment. People take on a different "affect," for instance, when they dress up to go out for a nice dinner or to a club. One might use terms like charismatic, inviting, dull, offensive, grotesque, shocking, attractive, elusive, horrifying, brilliant, mundane, or wholesome to describe something's affect. The specific quality is completely variable. What matters is that some quality seems to pervade the whole experience and is revealed through sense perception to a viewer and then elicits a response, whether it be a smile, a gasp, a shrug, or an embrace.

The way to analyze affect is through quality, valence, and arousal. **Quality** names the dominant quality that the thing possesses in that particular encounter, labeled with a highly specific term as the ones listed above. **Valence** refers to the positive or negative orientation of that quality as it is received by the viewer. Negative valence is associated with some form of pain and usually repels someone from the object. For instance, a joke may have the quality of being cruel and crude; for some people this may have a positive valence if it reflects their own biases, while others feel it has a negative valence to the extent that they would walk away and ask that it not be expressed. **Arousal** refers to the degree that affects are felt to be weak or powerful as an experience. For instance, seeing news coverage of the Cabbage Patch Riots may produce a low arousal of curiosity and disgust, while actually being present at the riots and seeing someone shoved to the ground would produce a strong reaction.

A mood, by contrast, is the exact opposite of affect. A **mood** is a pervasive feeling experienced by a person that seems not related at all to external objects, but rather originates within the self and pervades an atmosphere. Moods, like the state of depression, stay the same regardless of one's situation. In fact, mood seems to "color" external objects with one's own emotions, as when someone in a joyous mood experiences everything positively, whereas a person in a paranoid mood perceives everything as hidden, dangerous, and not what it seems. Mood is more deeply psychological than affect. A mood tends to be a product both the biology and character of the individual as well as the long-term qualities of one's environment. Certainly, a community suffering war, poverty, hunger, and discrimination may have pervasive and shared moods of despair, while successful, secure, and powerful communities tend toward positive moods that are hopeful for the future.

The main instruments of propaganda, however, are emotions. The parents who drove across three states to stand in long lines overnight to purchase a Cabbage Patch Kid were motivated by more than just the affect of the doll itself. The doll was situated within the wider, deeper, and more complex relationship between parent, child, and society. The desire, fear, guilt, and anger suffered by those parents was complex and tied up with memories of the past, expectations of the future, and ideals of how a good parent is supposed to behave. In other words, the emotions they felt were the product of a narrative understanding of themselves as players within a complicated human drama. The competitors who were hoarding Cabbage Patch Kids were seen as opponents and villains, the stores were like castles to be stormed, and the image of their happy child on Christmas morning was a utopia. Unlike affect, which seems to emanate from the object, emotions arise within a relationship between an actor in some aspect of his or her environment that is undergoing change. Emotions respond to environmental conditions as forms of intuitive judgment and incipient action, helping us navigate our terrain by telling us what to strive for, what to let go, what to hold onto, and what to fight against.

In sum, **emotions** are dramatized feelings accompanied by pain and pleasure that orient individuals to objects, actions, events, and people within situations marked by change and that contain an implicit judgment. The phrase "dramatized feelings" is meant to highlight both the physical, sensory component of emotions as well as their cognitive component. We literally "feel" emotions in our body, both in terms of the sensory input we receive as well as our physical response such as the tightening of our chests for the quickening of our hearts. We have these feelings because we have cognitively processed their situation in such a way that we have placed ourselves within a drama. Think, for instance, of an isolated sound, like the scraping of a boot on the floor. Now picture this sound faintly approaching on the other side of a closed door that you are huddled behind, in the dark, gripping a screwdriver in self-defense. Who is approaching? And what are you prepared to do? This is how a feeling is "dramatized" into an emotion. Also, these emotions always are accompanied by a mixture of pleasure and pain. Imagine a graduation ceremony. A parent is proud of their child's accomplishment, which brings pleasure, and yet experiences pain in knowing they will be moving away and starting a new, independent life. Finally, emotions apply judgments, which is to say assertions of value, definition, and action. To be offended at a dirty joke is to declare it an inappropriate expression without even having to say so. To see a person approaching and feel joy, anxiety, distrust, fear, or surprise is to make an immediate judgment that determines our future behavior of whether to greet them or avoid them.

The dramatic quality of our motions is crucial to understanding how propaganda manipulates emotions for its own purposes. Propaganda after all does not make use of emotional appeal simply by telling people to feel this or that emotion. It uses emotions by narrating events in such a way that the audience is situated within a drama in which the emotion arises quite naturally. This chapter is called "arousing passions" for this reason. A "passion" is a kind of emotion that we feel we "suffer," which is to say something that seems to happen to us and rises up against our will. To "arouse" a "passion" is like stoking the fire; it places a person within a situation in which they can't seem to help themselves. They *must* have that thing (desire), or hate that person (anger), or feel ashamed at what they have done (guilt), or flee from some terror (fear). Propaganda attempts to surround an audience with impressions that make them feel driven by necessity to act in a certain way. Returning to our conception of motives of short answer situations, propaganda seems to dramatize a situation in which even the most inflamed passion seems to be the appropriate response.

DESIRE

For many locations around the world, over-tourism has become a problem. A *Business Insider* article gives a few examples. In Pembrokeshire, Wales, the city has asked fans of the *Harry Potter* series to stop leaving socks at the memorial site of the house elf Dobby. Since 2015, more than a million people have visited Iceland's Fjadrárgljúfur Canyon and damaged the fragile landscape in their eagerness to experience the place where Jon Snow battled zombie hordes in *Game of Thrones*. The medieval monastery on Skellig Michael, an island in County Kerry, Ireland, far exceeded its tourist limit after being featured in two *Star Wars* films, threatening the monastic remains and putting its famous birds at risk. And the beach on Maya Bay, a cove on the Thai island of Phi Phi Leh, had to be shut down indefinitely after 5,000 descended on the beach daily after being featured in Leonardo DiCaprio's 2000 film *The Beach*.[2] In each case, some real-life location featured in a fictional movie became a pilgrimage site for eager fans, often boosting the local economy while doing damage to the very thing that attracted visitors in the first place. In many cases, like Maya Bay, these sites are quite literally loved to death.

The rising popularity of "film tourism" presents a case study in the way that propaganda is able to create desire. The film industry, of course, might be considered sociological propaganda insofar as it is in the business of romanticizing certain places, cultures, and ways of life, whether fictional or real. In each of the cases above, the films created a universe of romance and adventure in which heroic characters played out fantasy dramas in exotic locations. Normally, such fictional worlds might exist only in the imagination. But in these films, some of the locations were real. This connection with reality offered fans an opportunity to experience a piece of that fictional world for themselves, often to rehearse the same actions on site as their favorite characters—as when fans of the movie *Joker* crowd the long stairway in the New York City neighborhood of the Bronx to dance down the steps and, in the process, obstruct and even endanger local residents. The movies and their on-location sets thus created in these fans a desire for travel and experience that would never have existed on its own. But once these locations appear in a movie, they are marked as objects of desire which turns them from places into destinations. What is unusual is that the locations are often not valued for their own sake, but because they allow the visitors to play out an imaginary fantasy. The desire is not for the place but for the fiction of the place.

Film tourism shows the power of propaganda to create desire out of almost anything. In its most general sense, **desire** is the active impulse to possess or experience something we perceive to be lacking. The term "active impulse" emphasizes the fact that desire moves us toward something and inspires action. Desire is different from mere wish or fantasy, which create attractive images of what "might be" but do not actually play a role in our choices. The presence of desire pushes us in one direction and not another and forces us to make sacrifices to satisfy our desires. And it is an "impulse" because desire often does not come with a clear reason. It sometimes quite literally just manifests as an urgent craving, often rooted in our biological nature. Second, desire seeks to "possess or experience" something, as one might possess a new home or experience the birth of a child. Desire thus seeks, at least metaphorically, to bring something close to itself. Desire takes the form of wanting "to have" or "to do." Finally, desire arises from something we "perceive to be lacking." I say "perception" because this lack may be tangibly felt and knowingly identified, otherwise it is not felt as a lack. Someone who has never seen *The Lord of the Rings* movies may have little desire to visit the Hobbiton film set just outside a small farming village in New Zealand. But once that lack is felt to be an absence, it creates an accompanying desire to fill that lack, even when the qualitative nature of fulfillment remains vague.

Propaganda arouses desires in a way that satisfies the propagandist goals by achieving three persuasive aims: 1) creation of a perceived lack; 2) image of an ideal future; and 3) presentation of an effective means. Although all three persuasive aims must somehow be present in any appeal to desire, a more sophisticated propagandist will often leave some of them unsaid. This usually occurs when some aspect of the message can be taken for granted and thus filled in by the audience. A beer commercial featuring good friends spending quality time together sharing stories over drinks need not specify the "lack" being filled or even showing how and why beer facilitates companionship. What matters is the creation of the desire for fulfillment. But in situations in which we seek the eradication of a problem rather than the attainment of an idealized future, the focus may turn on the means of action. A skin cream that promises to cure acne may only briefly show a clean complexion but spend most of the time explaining the functioning of the product versus competitors. Or perhaps the issue is to create desire making a problem feel more salient. A politics of agitation may emphasize primarily the "lack" of a secure, prosperous, and equitable society in the hope that voters will opt for the party out of power simply for a change, regardless of their policies or promises. But these latter two tactics diminish the motivational influence of desire to a minimum, replacing it instead with fear or anger, as will be explained in the next sections. Desire is most prominent, therefore, when it follows the pattern of the first examples by focusing on the active impulse for an idealized future so that desire draws one forward rather than being pushed from behind.

Despite the fact that desire itself is a universal part of the human condition, what and how people desire varies widely and remains a very mysterious and unpredictable affair. Any glance at the history of fashion reveals how quickly fads and trends come and go, often without a clear cause. There are, however, some general features that are common to objects of mass desire that provide a framework for invention and analysis. Some of these include being sensual, novel, unexpected, scarce, authentic, powerful, imaginable, and exclusive. For instance, virtually any object of desire must have a *sensual* quality insofar as it has a material manifestation that pleases the senses in some way or is seen as a means of gratifying the senses. *Authenticity* means a sense that what is desired "fits" one's identity and is a natural extension of themselves. To be *imaginable* means that people in this group can literally envision themselves possessing or experiencing this thing in actual life rather than a fantasy. *Novelty* may be just a newer model of a familiar product, such as a new smartphone with a better camera or a new flavor of holiday coffee. That which is *unexpected* seems to come out of the blue and has a more dramatic novelty that often comes with a sense of risk or danger. Desire also tends to focus on things that promise to increase one's *power*, meaning here the ability to act with confidence in a practical or social setting. A cleaning product can be desired for power as much as an ideology. Lastly, that which is desired usually has some aspect of scarcity to increase its desirability. *Scarcity* means the quality of not being readily available without considerable effort to attain it, as in the social heuristic that tells us that what is scarce, or hard to attain, is also that which is desirable for others. The fact that exotic movie sets satisfy almost all of these qualities is the reason they are such enduring destinations.

A tactic that arouses desire exists as an active impulse only within a delicate balance between presence, absence, and fulfillment. A desire, to be desired, must be fully present to the imagination (arousal) with the promise of sensual reward that draws us closer to it (positive valence). In propaganda, this presence is most often achieved through visual representation combined with symbolic description. For instance, imagine the picture of a parent taking pleasure in witnessing their child curled up with a Cabbage Patch Kid as she drifts off to sleep. At the same time, however, desires are more forceful when that which is desired is tangibly absent. This absence creates the lack which creates an urge for satisfaction, driving those same parents to an anxious frenzy to purchase the doll at all costs. Finally, desire must at some point be able to be fulfilled in a meaningful way in order to make the quest worthwhile. A desire forever deferred becomes a mere fantasy and at worst creates an angry backlash against it. In propaganda, of course, any fulfillment is never the satiation of desire but the beginning of another one. Propaganda rarely wants people to rest content with what they have. Propaganda in this way thrives in the restless pursuit of the next desire, always getting people to pursue the next model, the next level, the new age, the better love, the more perfect body, the more powerful empire, or the greater good. Consequently, propaganda as a technique always tends toward a model based on addiction, in which desire is always present but never fully satisfied. At its best, it creates the incentive for growth. At its worst, propaganda promises happiness but always manages to sow discontent.

FEAR

In July, 2021, the Australian government released an advertisement intended to shock its viewers into action. The 30-second television spot was very simple. A black screen gives way to the sound of desperate gasping for air and we see a terrified face of a young woman on an oxygen respirator in a hospital bed. The camera is positioned directly over her face, as if the viewer was leaning over the bed. The colors are a pale, washed-out green in high contrast, conveying a cold, clinical feel. As the woman gasps, her eyes look around frantically for help as her hands uselessly move to her face as if they could help her breathe. But no one is there to comfort or to aid her. She lays there, helpless, terrified, and alone, as her body desperately fights off suffocation. After 20 seconds of this agony, the screen fades to black and we see the words "COVID-19 can affect anyone." Then another blank screen appears followed by three instructions, one after the other: "Stay home." "Get tested." "Book your vaccination." The final slide shows the website Australia.gov.au and phone number 1-800-020-080. Finally, the ad closes with the phrase "COVID-19 VACCINATION Keeping Australia COVIDSAFE."

This commercial, released in 2021 after development of the first COVID vaccine, came out a year and a half after the pandemic began in January, 2020. So it was not the first fear appeal used in response to the outbreak. Nor was the object of fear in these other appeals always the same. There had been and would be many other fears to go around besides the fear of getting infected with the virus. For instance, because the outbreak had originated in Wuhan, China, fear of the virus in the early months was transferred to fear of anyone perceived to be Chinese, whether those people had been to China or not. The location of a nearby disease research lab also aroused fear that the virus was a form of biological warfare, soon to get worse. The enactment of lockdown quarantine measures brought out the fear of lacking basic necessities, which led to confrontations at supermarkets over the last remaining stocks of toilet paper. These incidents, in turn, created fears of general anarchy and martial law, which made personal gun sales skyrocket as homeowners prepared to defend themselves against rioters and looters. Conspiracies were also quick to interpret lockdown measures as part of a preplanned government takeover of all civil life, ushering in a new totalitarian state. And even after the vaccine was created and made available, many people refused to get them out of fear that the vaccines themselves were dangerous or, at worst, or part of a government-sponsored tracking mechanism. And everywhere there was simply the shared fear that enforced isolation was taking away moments in one's life that could never be taken back, as when students missed their senior years and graduations, while others were prevented from visiting sick loved ones out of fear of contagion. Yet, despite all of these fears (and in many ways because of them) social life continued on, measures were implemented and followed, and eventually the pandemic was over.

COVID-19 is an ideal case study to introduce the tactic of fear because it shows both the necessity of fear appeals to motivate mass action as well as their dangerous exploitability. On the one hand, global coordination of a response to the virus would be impossible without fear appeals. Only by masses of people acting in concert to self-regulate their behaviors to avoid infection were governments able to prevent millions more deaths. And that constitution of collective agency was only possible because the majority of people feared putting themselves and their loved ones in danger. On the other hand, atmospheres of fear are easily exploited by people to serve their own interests, as occurred during the explosion of quick fixes peddled by marketeers or conspiracy theorists. This double characteristic of fear as a source of both protection and victimization is intrinsic to the emotion itself. Fear exists to protect us from harm, but once aroused it tends to attach itself impulsively to what is near at hand in a way that can itself be more self-destructive than what is being feared.

To understand the basis of fear, it is helpful to think of fear in survivalist, evolutionary terms. Fear originates as a more complex emotional state than mere sense perception and reaction for organisms that must navigate more complex environments than plants or insects. If humans had evolved in an environment in which a certain stimulus always indicated danger, then instinct alone would react to that stimulus without the need for intervening emotion. It would simply occur, much as a loud noise in the dark makes us jump. But fear is more than just a flight response. As an emotion, fear "sizes up" a situation, reads the signs as danger signs, pinpoints a possible cause, and places us in an attitude that prepares us to act without itself *determining* the act. If fear always led directly to a flight or attack response, then military self-discipline would be impossible. In other words, fear is both an affective as well as a cognitive process of interpreting a situation in a certain way. But our practical judgment remains independent of this emotion and may "override" it when it deems it worth the risk. The status of emotion as a form of preliminary judgment, as a way of seeing the situation without determining the exact response, thus helps higher animals, including human beings, respond with greater foresight and complexity than sheer instinct. Indeed, many of our judgments are made by comparing two or more fears and deciding which is the greater. Fear is not an irrational emotion. One could argue, in fact, that it is the *most* rational, at least when aroused within the right conditions.

We can define **fear** as the unpleasant emotion caused by the anticipation of harm that will bring pain and suffering to oneself and the people one cares about. Fear can thus be said to be a product of three variables: harm, proximity, and care. If any one of these three variables are missing, then fear appeals usually miss their target. First, fear can only be produced when a specific *harm* is vividly described capable of being imagined as causing significant pain, physical or emotional. The graphic close-up of a young woman gasping for air makes it perfectly clear that potential harm of COVID-19. Second, this harm must be *proximate* enough that it may actually happen, thus bringing the harm close rather than some far-off impossibility. In the case of the COVID-19 video, proximity hardly needed to be shown at the time due to the global pandemic, but in its very early stages the virus was not experienced by most US citizens directly and hence was easy to put out of mind as something only happening in China. Lastly, this proximate harm must affect someone one *cares* about, including oneself. If, for instance, young people are convinced that COVID-19 won't affect them very much, they will not respond with fear even though they may feel sympathy for others. The tactic of the Australian government's COVIDSAFE video is to pierce the armor of youthful confidence by making the sufferer a *young* woman to show that harm may come to them, too. Once all three variables are satisfied, a fear response is usually inevitable.

Of the three variables in fear, the one that most determines what people actually fear is care. But this requires being more specific than simply identifying the person or group that might be harmed. Care also includes the *aspect* of that person or group one cares most about. For a propagandist, this determination often requires lengthy demographic study and analysis, today often scraped from available data online among particular research habits. But much about what people fear the most can be intuited from common sense in everyday experience. Young, single people typically fear social stigma, loneliness, failure, while parents fear for the safety of their children, financial security, or loss of a job. One could do the same brainstorming for any demographic, no matter how broadly or narrowly construed. Many vitamins, drinks, bandages, creams, or braces are sold to athletes, for instance, based on their fear of career ending injury. High fashion thrives off the fear of wealthy and popular socialites of dressing out of style. Religions for all times have existed to calm fears of death through reassurance of some afterlife. And politicians regularly propose policies that promise to meet the threat of some looming disaster, whether through aggressive violence or benign social policy. But just because religion and politics may deal with seemingly "serious" fears on a large scale does not mean they always represent the greatest fear. A teenager whose face breaks out with acne before the big dance is far more terrified by their visage in the mirror than they are about poverty, climate change, and war. Not only is fear relative to one's position in life, but also what we *should* fear often has very little to do with what we *actually* fear.

As a tactic of propaganda designed to direct action, fear must also be proportionate to the self-confidence of the audience to avoid either paralysis or neglect. One of the challenges of any fear appeal is knowing how much one should scare one's audience. Too graphically imagining an extremely frightening and dangerous outcome often has the effect of turning away an audience that isn't prepared to deal with that level of fear. Perhaps it is simply too horrifying to look at, thereby making them literally not see what is represented, or perhaps the audience understands the situation but feels helpless against the magnitude of the threat, so they choose fatalism or simply denial. On the other hand, too mild a representation fails to break through the consciousness of people as something urgent that needs to be addressed. When people aren't actually scared they put the issue aside or simply ignore it altogether as not frightening enough to bother with. What determines the degree of fear to be used is the self-confidence of the receiver to deal with the threat, both in terms of their individual capacities as well as their access to resources. It is no accident that philanthropists are often very successful business people with higher education, self-esteem, money, resources, and reputation. Hence, they see confronting major threats as a badge of honor. Those with few resources, skills, education, or time tend to focus on immediate problems that can be overcome with what is at hand. Faced with a pandemic, those with greater resources tended to throw themselves into designing large-scale solutions, while busy parents focused on regularly wearing a mask at the store and maybe signing up for a free vaccine when it was made available.

Finally, the appeals must present a solution to fear that is understandable, accessible, and easily acted upon. In the case of the Australian COVID-19 video, the high fear appeal of the suffocating patient is paired with a very simple path to protecting oneself—signing up for a free vaccine. No matter how severe, complex, or enormous the problem, propaganda provokes action by clearing a path to some effective action that is proven to be within the reach of the audience. Anything that requires a more complex response with many steps over time and space ceases to be propaganda and becomes a policy position understood by central route processing. This does not necessarily make the two approaches competitors, although it often does in practice. On the one hand, the action provoked by a fear appeal can create an interest that leads to a more complex involvement in an organizational policy. Fear appeals may spark immediate interest but then turn into a lifelong commitment to combating a serious global threat, as when fear of the ozone hole in the atmosphere produced sustained global cooperation.[3] On the other hand, fear appeals are easily used to distract people from larger systemic challenges and focus them on what are often trivial or even nonexistent threats. The most frequently exploited fear appeal, for instance, is simply fear of other people, as already seen in the discussion of how fear of Syrian refugees was used to promote Brexit. In Poland, for instance, an ironically titled "Propaganda Law" (because it was passed to "fight" propaganda) prohibited any "depiction and promotion" of "diverse gender identities and sexual orientations" out of a vague fear that LGBTI groups are trying to brainwash young people into a "gay agenda." Amnesty International's findings "indicate that the law is unduly restricting people's right to freedom of expression, including children's right to access information, in a manner that is neither provided by law, nor necessary or proportionate."[4] Once again, however, anti-propaganda propaganda successfully created fear of covert mass manipulation to impose state censorship on a wide swath of public discourse, which resulted, of course, in the further spread of fear.

When taken to the extreme, the fear appeal can therefore easily turn into **terrorism**, which occurs when fear is intentionally overwhelming so that it produces a mood of terror that paralyzes all action and reduces the power to act in concert. Terror, unlike fear, is not object-oriented but atmospheric, closer to a mood. Terror comes from anywhere and nowhere, so that one never knows where fear might strike. For many authors, for instance, Poland's law generated such an atmosphere. One Polish writer Dóra Papp told Amnesty International how she was threatened on social media in a way that she had not experienced before the passing of the law: "It has taken a toll on me. After so many years of signings when it was a pleasure to meet readers, fear was planted in me, because I didn't know how seriously to take the threat."[5] Terrorists and terroristic laws use this tactic to break apart the cooperative unity of the society which makes it easier to divide and conquer. But even domestic policies can use a form of terrorism when it presents "internal" threats, such as immigrants or foreign agents or other minority religious groups, as if they were insidious threats to the social order. This type of threat generates forms of distrust, paranoia, and hate while putting forth solutions that only further exaggerates an atmosphere of terror. Especially in the digital age, when any threat can be manufactured using graphic manipulation and disinformation, the ease by which fear appeals spread has been greatly increased as a result. Genuine threats like a pandemic can quickly be exploited to manufacture a form of terror that makes people paranoid, angry, desperate, easily susceptible to magical cures and hate speech. Fear must be used when society faces genuine threats, that much is clear. But it is equally true that no society can exist for long in a state of terror.

GUILT

In 2004, the company BP (British Petroleum) released a television advertisement titled "carbon footprint." The video begins with a simple white background on which appears a small star-shaped BP logo and a simple question: "what size is your carbon footprint?" The ad then transitions to four person-on-the-street interviews with what seem to be ordinary British citizens. The first confesses ignorance of the term, the second said he doesn't know but he imagines that globally it must be a very large number, the third guesses that it is "how much carbon I produce," and the last—a confident young man leaning against the rail of a bridge—says "you mean the effect that my living has on the earth in terms of the products I consume?" The white screen then returns the words "we can all do more to emit less." After mentioning a plan to reduce emissions by 4 million tons, the commercial makes a call to action: "Learn to lower your carbon footprint at bp.com/carbonfootprint." Then: "it's a start." Finally, the logo appears with the new rebranding of BP: "Beyond petroleum."[6]

Until the appearance of this ad, the concept of the carbon footprint was unknown. There did exist the notion of the "ecological footprint" that had been developed in 1992 and which referred to how many environmental resources were required to support a specific way of life or business. But in 2003, BP hired the public relations firm Ogilvy & Mather to promote the idea that climate change, which is the result of carbon dioxide in the atmosphere, was more a product of individual behavior than the fault of the oil industry or other major manufacturing interests. BP thus altered the idea of the ecological footprint to become the carbon footprint, which specifically referred to how much carbon was produced to support a person's lifestyle and consumer choices. As part of their campaign rollout, they unveiled a "carbon footprint calculator" (placed in the commercial in its hyperlink) that people could use to assess how much carbon they used in daily life, from commuting to eating food to heating our house to purchasing clothes or engaging in leisure activities. Their rebranding of BP as "beyond petroleum" was part of this campaign, indicating that the oil giant was now committed to reducing the need for its own signature product by convincing its own consumers to cut down on their "footprints." By shifting responsibility to the individual consumer, BP could thus relieve itself of responsibility for climate change while simultaneously presenting itself as a leader in educating the public in environmental ethics.

The remarkable success of this cliché is due, in part, to the simple fact that it is both mathematically calculable and also based in fact. Regardless of its propagandistic origins, the notion of the carbon footprint does actually capture and high-spot the real impact that our consumption practices have on carbon production, whether due to direct burning of fuels and transportation or due to the indirect burning of resources to produce or dispose of commodities. It also led to the marketing of the idea of "carbon neutral" practices and products, with entire organizations and even cities seeking to become carbon neutral, in which the amount of carbon used is offset by removals of carbon from the atmosphere. These clichés can then be used both to praise and to condemn. Take, for instance, climate activist Greta Thunberg, well-known for mobilizing a generation of young people to engage in climate activism. When she wished to attend the 2019 UN climate action Summit in New York City, she opted not to fly from Europe because of the carbon footprint of the airline industry. Instead, she boarded a racing yacht to cross the Atlantic.[7] But this action also opened the door for criticism to blame her for every other flight she had ever taken, thus allowing people to accuse her of hypocrisy for creating a large carbon footprint that was accumulated in the name of reducing carbon emissions.[8]

But the propaganda tactic behind the success of the carbon footprint was, fundamentally, guilt. People acted because the cliché made them feel personally responsible for harming the planet and they wished to redeem themselves in their own eyes and the eyes of others. Of course, this mechanism is just another form of the rationalization trap, which is absolutely central to any guilt appeal. And because guilt, in some form, is almost always present in more complex propaganda tactics in some way, the rationalization trap is also present. Put simply, guilt is the unpleasant feeling of having committed an offense and engaged in some wrongdoing. We thus feel guilt when we fail to live up to some ideal, principle, or standard that we hold valuable and which has resulted in some harm, however intangible that harm might be. Greta Thunberg, for instance, sailed on a carbon-neutral yacht trip so that she would not feel guilty for increasing emissions to receive an award for advocating for lower emissions. The harm implied, however, was not simply the material effects of increased carbon in the atmosphere, but also the harm done to her own personal integrity and her relations to others if she felt she were being manipulative or hypocritical. What matters in guilt is not the nature of the harm itself but the feeling of having done wrong, even if the harm was purely to one's own sense of dignity and pride.

Guilt is in many ways the most complex of the four motions being studied here because of its triadic nature. **Guilt** is the painful feeling of wrongdoing in which people feel to have judged their actions to be some violation of a deeply held value. To produce a feeling of guilt, therefore, three things must be present at one time—a value, a violation, and a judgment. A **value** is any image of an ideal action or event that might be captured in a principle, law, or definition that is actively sought after and treasured by an individual. For instance, to value "personal responsibility" is to take pleasure in seeing oneself as perceiving a problem and taking the initiative to address it through one's own individual agency and not waiting for others to fix it. A **violation** is a specific act that has either contradicted or at least not lived up to the standard of the value. I say "violation" and not simply "act" because an action must be consciously perceived as being related to a value for it to become a violation. Before the cliché of the "carbon footprint" was made popular, climate activists might not have consciously felt that flying by plane to a climate conference in any way violated their values. Lastly, a **judgment** is a determination by oneself that this violation was not justified or excusable. The difference between violation and judgment is important because it translates the action into emotion. Often, people can tolerate and dismiss violations when they go unnoticed by others or when individuals are able to convince themselves, through various forms of resolving cognitive dissonance, that it wasn't really a big deal. Often it is the presence of some external judge one respects, in particular friends and family, that turns violations into judgments. A violation is a mere accusation. The judgment pronounces one guilty in the moral court of one's conscience. The desire to avoid this verdict forced Greta Thunberg, after all, to cross the Atlantic in a boat.

One can think of the guilt appeal in propaganda more accurately as the arousal of guilt to make the target feel they must do something specific by pointing to a particular action that serves as a vehicle for redemption. By "redemption," I mean a publicly recognizable action that is seen to "make up" for past failure and therefore improve one's commitment to the value. Redemption can come in two forms. Redemption either involves disciplining the self, which is called "mortification," or punishing someone or something outside oneself, which is called "blame." In other words, when one feels guilty, one must then find something to point to as cause for the violation. Sometimes this cause is found inside oneself, as one might feel guilty for a desire to keep one's house cool which leads to an increase in air-conditioning usage which increases one's carbon footprint. Mortification would suppress this desire to always feel comfortable and show redemption by swearing off air-conditioning for good. Other times, redemption can occur by actively blaming others and seeking to enact a kind of justice upon it or upon them by confronting that which caused the problem in the first place. An energy regulator who took bribes to allow the industry to spew excess pollutants must therefore pair mortification (to plead guilty and admit one's own fault) with an outward commitment to join an environmental group seeking to block offshore drilling rigs by a rapacious oil company (therefore also expending energy to attack an external threat). Redemption, as we saw in the previous discussion of ethos, usually involves some combination of mortification and blame.

Propaganda successfully makes use of guilt when it manages, directly or indirectly, to connect all three qualities of guilt and then propose an action that promises redemption. Take, for instance, the Nike cliché "Just Do It" that we have already discussed. The slogan is thoroughly imbued with guilt. Had the cliché been "Go for It!" then it primarily would have aroused desire. But "Just Do It" is a phrase said with a connotation of frustration and impatience. Clearly, the target of this cliché had already articulated a goal that expressed the highest value. This individual has raised the bar and set their sights for success. But instead of pursuing that goal, they have failed to act, making excuses and not living up to their word. They are all talk and no action. "Just Do It" draws a line in the sand and says that this person should either put up or shut up. Already the viewer is guilty in the eyes of the cliché. The question is whether that person is going to go through a process of mortification, put down their doubts and fears, and take a chance. And when they do, Nike and its products will be there to help. Indeed, even taking the step to buy a Nike product is itself a form of redemption, being the first publicly recognizable step that one has, in fact, decided to live their highest values.

Finally, consider one of the most iconic political slogans of the first quarter of the 21st century, President Donald Trump's "Make

America Great Again" (MAGA for short). Although the phrase has been used by several past presidents, Trump's 2016 campaign gave it a prominent and an emotional power that it never had before, most notably expressed in all caps on bright red baseball hats.[9] Trump's use of this cliché channeled the force of guilt into political power. Had he said "Let's Make America Great!" this would have activated the desire for a possible future. But the phrasing "great *again*" implies a fall from greatness and a desire to return to a previous state. Not surprisingly, Trump's political messaging often focused on the negative, emphasizing all of the facets of decline he saw characterizing America as failing. This gap between America's past greatness and present carnage implied failure across the board to wholesale violations of value leading to a damning judgment not only of the United States political class but also the voters who elected them. Trump thus cast himself as the redemption for the country, with voters redeeming themselves by supporting his campaign and electing him to office.

What is often neglected when considering the guilt appeal is the degree to which its effectiveness is actually based on self-respect and pride. We often consider guilt as something that applies only to the guilty, which is to say criminals. But as we have seen, criminals in a formal sense may not experience guilt at all if they do not profess the same values as those who judge them. The most extreme guilt is that expressed by those individuals and groups who hold themselves to the highest of ideals. For those seeking perfection but who stumble or fail on the road to greatness, guilt is experienced very deeply and powerfully. As indicated by the Trump campaign slogan, guilt is keenly felt when someone who had once experienced (or thought they had experienced) a taste of perfection in the past but then falls from grace and judges their present low state by the past heights. Gyms, for instance, have consistently attracted patrons who were once youthful athletes in high school and college and are constantly feeling guilty when they judge themselves by their past physique. That is why guilt is often resolved not through acts of redemption, but by changing the formula. As old age, for instance, makes past glories impossible, one way of adjusting is to change the values by which one regulates one's life. To accept one's limitations is to focus on the values that are actually possible to attain and which can still bring some good into the world.

ANGER

In 2013, one of the most widely recognized social media hashtags of the early 21st century was invented by three Black women organizers, Alicia Garza, Patrisse Cullors, and Opal Tometi. This was #BlackLivesMatter. These three women developed the hashtag and organized the corresponding political movement as a response to the acquittal of George Zimmerman for the shooting death of Trayvon Martin. The death of Martin had attracted national attention for shocking brutality. Martin, a Black 17-year-old young man who had accompanied his father to visit his father's fiancée at her townhouse, was walking back to her home after buying Skittles candy at a convenience store. A member of the neighborhood watch, George Zimmerman, reported Martin as suspicious to the police, but instead of waiting for them to arrive, he confronted Martin and shot him in the chest. Martin was unarmed except for a bag of candy, so it seemed clear to anyone in the Black community that Zimmerman had committed a murder motivated largely by racism. But a court found him innocent, accepting Zimmerman's justification of self-defense—this despite the fact that it was Zimmerman who had approached Martin with a gun. The hashtag #BlackLivesMatter was thus a direct response to both an act of racist violence and a courtroom decision that appeared to say that Black lives didn't seem to matter to the criminal justice system.

At the center of the Black Lives Matter movement was a righteous anger at systemic injustice. According to the founders of the movement on their website: "Black Lives Matter became the rallying cry in the fight to end white supremacy, anti-Black systemic racism, and the brutality inflicted on black people at the hands of the state and local law enforcement."[10] This highly focused anger led to arguably the greatest wave of global protests in the subsequent years that the world had ever witnessed, driven by the decentralized organizing capacity of social media and local groups. That the driving emotion was anger was argued by Yolanda Pierce, a professor and dean of the Howard University school of divinity. Pierce argued that Black Lives Matter is a movement that "unapologetically embraces righteous anger and passionate possibilities." She asks: "Why are you not angry at the death of a 12-year-old black child playing in the park, at the hands of law enforcement?" For Pierce, therefore, emotions like anger have a role to play in social change: "The prophetic work of 'turning over the tables' and fighting against the forces of injustice requires the complete range of human capacity, including love, anger, hope, joy, and even moments of despair."[11] But when confronted with the evils of the world, anger is usually the first to turn the tables.

This example demonstrates how anger is used in propaganda in four ways. First, #BlackLivesMatter shows how there is no clear distinction between the persuasive tactics of a social movement and that of propaganda. All social movements employ tools of mass persuasion and therefore should be studied using the same conceptual vocabulary as any other campaign. Second, this case study indicates how anger is far more a factor in social and political propaganda than it is in consumer marketing, in which desire and fear tend to dominate. But where serious problems are confronted in propaganda that directly impact people's lives for the worst, anger is never far behind. Third, the reformist tenor of Black Lives Matter challenges the frequent assumption that anger in propaganda is always a negative, oppressive emotion connected more with racist regimes than with the fight against racism. But anger can play an important righteous function for those who feel indignation at some injustice. Lastly, the very cliché #BlackLivesMatter has emotional anger built into its very grammar. Reacting to systemic violence against Black people in society, it accuses those in power of not caring about Black lives. The assertion that Black lives "matter" accuses those who directly cause harm to Black lives of not seeming to care. It is a wholesale condemnation of systemic racial injustice.

Anger is an emotion characterized by antagonism toward someone or something that you perceive has deliberately done you or someone you care about harm. Anger thus has three components—harm, cause, and intention. In other words, anger must perceive some actual or impending harm to oneself or someone one cares about, attribute that harm to a specific cause, and see the source of that cause as intending that harm. Just as with guilt, therefore, the absence of any one of these three factors will not provoke anger. Harm done to some far-off group by an admittedly evil actor may evoke sympathy but not necessarily anger. Harm that is directly experienced purely accidentally or naturally, such as a hurricane or tripping on a rock, does not make us angry at those things. Or if a person is experiencing intense physical pain, but does not know the cause of it, the anger has nowhere to attach itself beyond a vague sense of frustration with not knowing why. Propaganda often exploits this frustration by channeling those feelings toward a common object that serves the interests of the propagandist.

Because of the causal logic behind anger, propaganda often pairs tactics of simplifying ideas with vivid appeals to generate an anger response. The paradigmatic case is the "atrocity story" which broadcasts a graphic account of some violent act against the sympathetic victim and then simplifies the motive to an evildoer seeking to oppress or exploit the victim for their own gain or pleasure. Propaganda of this type often appears in the digital format of visual image plus caption, which fits the social media genre of communication perfectly. In the context of #BlackLivesMatter, the video of the death of George Floyd, a Black man who suffocated to death after a Minneapolis police officer Derek Chauvin knelt on his neck for nine minutes and 29 seconds, sparked one of the most widespread protests ever witnessed in the United States. His dying words, "I can't breathe," became a powerful cliché that captured what many felt to be the conditions living under police brutality.[12] But vivid appeals can also be completely fabricated, as in the case of the frequently recounted story leading up to the 1991 Gulf War in which a young woman purported to see Iraqi soldiers killing newborn babies in Kuwaiti hospitals. It was later revealed that the young woman had been coached by a public relations firm prior to her testimony, that she was actually the daughter of the Kuwaiti ambassador, and that she had never worked in a hospital.[13] But the anger produced by her testimony was used to justify U.S. military intervention.

Anger is a potent emotion precisely because it has a way of pulling all the other emotions into it. We are angry when our desires are thwarted, when we seek to blame others for our guilt, and when we seek to punish that which makes us fear. Anger and fear appeals are often found together, in fact, although fear is intentionally kept at a low enough level to mobilize aggressive action. Too much fear stimulates a flight reaction or results in terror, both of which overwhelm the directed character of anger. But not enough fear results in a rather dismissive attitude that does not take the violation seriously. The fear, therefore, can often appear in the form of the hypothetical question: "What if we do nothing?" And this question also activates forms of guilt. Anger thus channels these other emotions and gives them a target—which also has the effect of activating a desire for a future without the presence of the offending person or object. Anyone acquainted with popular movies of heroic under-dogs fighting villainous bullies should be familiar with this nexus of emotions, in which fear gives rise to guilt, and guilt transforms the anger before achieving its desire. Even more problematically, we see fears of mere "possible" futures (rather than actual events or action) being the cause of anger against minority populations, resulting his-torically in pogroms based almost entirely on the logic of scape-goating and the fear of the Other. Thus, despite being at essence a simple emotion that often responds with knee-jerk immediacy to perceived violations, it can also be a much broader motion that car-ries other emotions along in its wake. And that is why wars can last for years or even decades and never run out of anger.

However well-intentioned anger appeals might be, therefore, they have just as much if not more susceptibility to being exploited, redirected, and magnified as fear does. That is because anger has a way of getting out of hand very quickly. To create anger, one must attribute some kind of ill intent to the doer of the deed and also show how the act was deliberate. This structure is in the very nature of the definition of murder. But in propaganda, there is no trial, evidence, or verdict. Whatever propaganda can make peo-ple believe becomes, for them, the truth. For instance, increased immigration in Ireland has led to an increase in nativist propaganda that blames crime, unemployment, and housing shortages on the presence of "foreigners." It only would take a single incident to spark violence: "So when social media rumours attributed a hor-rific stabbing attack on three children and a creche worker to a for-eigner – Algerian, Moroccan, Romanian, versions varied – groups descended on Parnell Square, the scene of the crime, and decided to unleash chaos." The result was the worst scene of violence in Dublin in years, with rioters attacking police, burning cars, and looting businesses to protest "foreigners" (never mind that the man who stopped the knife attack was a Brazilian Deliveroo rider).[14] But anger appeals like this almost always simplify a situation to highlight only the seemingly one-directional motives of causing harm, thus creating a one-dimensional caricature of an entire group that needs to be punished and purged.

But the fact that anger can be so easily exploited by tactical disinformation does not undermine the practical usefulness of anger as a tool of persuasion. Anger remains an essential emotion to any form of political activism. Groups like the Southern Poverty Law Center focus anger at hate-groups who constantly seek to sow division and instigate violence in order to empower publics and states to protect marginalized populations.[15] Anger at the systematic exploitation of women, children, and laborers across the globe is used to appeal to the justice of international law, as exemplified in a recent headline that exposed the existence of a literal slave market in Libya that read: "Libya migrant 'slave market' footage sparks outrage."[16] Anger at the exploitation of natural resources leading to the collapse of entire ecosystems drives the critique of unfettered development, as indicated by the news headline: "Anger is most powerful emotion by far for spurring climate action, study finds."[17] Within the constant tumult of public discourse, one can only hope to counter messages of irrational hate with ideals of righteous anger that makes possible some form of equitable justice and the possibility of peace.

WHY EMOTIONS ARE RATIONAL

There is good reason to be skeptical of emotional appeals in propaganda. The most notorious instances of propaganda often play on emotions, undermine rationality, appeal to biases, stoke hatred, and make us terrified with fear. Under the sway of such propaganda people seem to quite literally lose their minds and become bundles of emotional reactions, sometimes pursuing their wildest desires and other times fleeing from their greatest fears. But this exaggerated description of emotions, so common in anti-propaganda propaganda, distorts the actual function of emotions in judgment. The fact is that emotional appeals are not essentially irrational. Quite the opposite, they are absolutely essential for making important ethical decisions. Without an appeal to emotions, we would not be able to distinguish important aspects of our environment from incidental ones. Artificial intelligence may be, in its strictly calculative capacities, the embodiment of a kind of objective rationality, but no human being would wish to hand over ethical decisions and judgments to a computer algorithm. Emotions are what binds us intimately to the world around us and make us care. Paradoxically, the criticism of emotional appeal in the name of central processing actually makes central route processing impossible. The only reason individuals engage in deep reflection is because they feel motivated by some connection to their lives and experiences. This motivation is emotional.

The important distinction, therefore, is not between propaganda that appeals to emotion and rational discourses that do not. It is between propaganda that exploits emotions for short-term arousal and self-interest and propaganda that uses emotion to direct public action, highlight pressing problems, and open up opportunities for deeper involvement in human affairs. The founders of the Black Lives Matter movement, for instance, created it to organize citizens into enacting that would involve long-term commitments to community development and local activism. Still, one must admit that once propaganda arouses passions, they are not so easily contained. Even the most well-intentioned campaign can easily have its emotional appeals hijacked by self-interests and turned to counterproductive ends. When this happens, however, the only thing the original campaigners can do is to produce more propaganda clarifying their aims and values. We do not correct for a negative emotion by eradicating it. We only make it diminish by arousing a different passion to take its place.

DISCUSSION QUESTIONS

1. When we say that some object is "imposing" or "beautiful" or "frightening" or any other term of affect, to what degree are we referring to properties that are intrinsic to that object and not imposed on it by the viewer? In other words, does affect have a real, substantial basis in reality, or it is purely a subjective state of mind? And can propaganda create affect out of nothing or must it have some objective basis?

2. The list of emotions included here (desire, fear, guilt, and anger) is admittedly a short one. List other emotions you think are often aroused in propaganda and construct your own definitions based on the structure of emotion. To what extent can these other emotions be created through combinations or described as variations of the four described in this book?

EXERCISES

1. Imagine an extraordinary action that you are asking another person to perform that would dramatically disrupt their current habits and set them on a new life course. Now consider how you would persuade this person to do this same action by using each of the four emotional appeals. Consider what other aspects of the situation you had to create in order to make each emotion work. What does this say about the relationship between emotions and situations?

2. Find a movie that features charismatic heroes and villains that use persuasion to motivate their followers. What emotions does each side rely upon? Is there a distinct difference in the types of emotions they use, or is it the same emotions but just different objects?

SUGGESTED READINGS

One of the most thorough treatments of the role of emotions in persuasion comes from the literature on social movements, specifically James Jasper's *The Art of Moral Protest: Culture, Biography, and Creativity in Social Movements*. My treatment of emotion is indebted to Jasper's work, and this book also shows how the discourses of propaganda and social movements have much to gain by their interaction.

Another resource for the study of emotions in movement in Manuel Castells' *Networks of Outrage and Hope: Social Movements in the Internet Age*. Castells applies his theory of the network society to social and revolutionary movements, focusing on the two emotions of hope (desire) and outrage (anger). But much of his study is actually a study of tactics of propaganda.

Although over 2,000 years old, Aristotle's *Rhetoric* still offers modern readers provocative insights into the working of emotions in persuasion. Despite criticizing the value of emotional appeal, Aristotle spends the majority of the book discussing emotions. His careful and practical definitions are oriented toward their use in rhetoric, so they are easily incorporated into a discussion of propaganda.

NOTES

1 Christopher Hoffman, "Cabbage Patch Kids Riots: 40-year anniversary of toy-induced pandemonium," WPDE News, November 24, 2023, https://wpde.com/news/nation-world/reliving-the-cabbage-patch-doll-craze-of-1983-zayre-walmart-dolls-mob-coleco-christmas-new-york.

2 Zoë Miller, "11 famous movie and TV locations that locals say have been ruined by tourists," *Business Insider*, November 3, 2022, https://www.businessinsider.com/famous-movie-and-tv-locations-ruined-by-tourism-2020-2.

3 "Rebuilding the ozone layer: how the world came together for the ultimate repair job," UN Environmental Program, September 15, 2021, https://www.unep.org/news-and-stories/story/rebuilding-ozone-layer-how-world-came-together-ultimate-repair-job.

4 "Hungary: Propaganda Law has "created cloud of fear" pushing LGBTI+ community into the shadows," Amnesty International, February 27, 2024, https://www.amnesty.org/en/latest/news/2024/02/hungarypropaganda-law-has-created-cloud-of-fear-pushing-lgbti-community-into-the-shadows/.

5 "Hungary: Propaganda Law has "created cloud of fear" pushing LGBTI+ community into the shadows," Amnesty International, February 27, 2024, https://www.amnesty.org/en/latest/news/2024/02/hungarypropaganda-law-has-created-cloud-of-fear-pushing-lgbti-community-into-the-shadows/.

6 "BP Ad: Carbon Footprint," https://www.youtube.com/watch?v=ywrZPypqSB4.

7 Igor Bastidas, "Worrying about your carbon footprint is exactly what big oil wants you to do," *The Guardian*, August 31, 2021, https://www.theguardian.com/environment/2019/aug/28/greta-thunberg-arrival-in-new-york-delayed-by-rough-seas.

8 Victor Morton, "Greta Thunberg carbon-reduced plan blown by flight of captain," *Washington Times*, December 1, 2019, https://www.washingtontimes.com/news/2019/dec/1/greta-thunberg-carbon-reduced-plan-blown-flight-ca/.

9 Emma Margolin, "'Make America great again'—who said it first?," NBC News, September 9, 2016, https://www.nbcnews.com/politics/2016-election/make-america-great-again-who-said-it-first-n645716.

10 "Proclamation: Black Lives Matter Day," Black Lives Matter, July 10, 2023, https://blacklivesmatter.com/blm-day/.

11 Yolanda Pierce, "Righteous anger, Black Lives Matter, and the legacy of King," Berkeley Center for Religion, Peace, and World Affairs, January 16, 2018, https://berkleycenter.georgetown.edu/responses/righteous-anger-black-lives-matter-and-the-legacy-of-king.

12 "'I can't breathe': The refrain that reignited a movement," Amnesty International, June 30, 2020.

13 Phillip Knightley, "The disinformation campaign," *The Guardian*, October 4, 2001, https://www.theguardian.com/education/2001/oct/04/socialsciences.highereducation.

14 Rory Carroll, "'Government is not listening': anger over immigration spills into riot on Dublin's streets," *The Guardian*, November 24, 2023, https://www.theguardian.com/world/2023/nov/24/anger-immigration-riot-dublin-ireland.

15 "Fighting Hate," SPLC, https://www.splcenter.org/fighting-hate.

16 "Libya migrant 'slave market' footage sparks outrage," BBC News, November 18, 2017, https://www.bbc.com/news/world-africa-42038451.

17 Ajit Niranjan, "Anger is most powerful emotion by far for spurring climate action, study finds," *The Guardian*, August 21, 2023, https://www.theguardian.com/environment/2023/aug/21/anger-is-most-powerful-emotion-by-far-for-spurring-climate-action-study-finds.

7

WILL PROPAGANDA SAVE US OR DESTROY US?

When we consider the fate of human civilization from the eyes of the individual in isolation, there seems every reason to think that it is doomed. Look at the human organism, born with the same archaic emotional and cognitive equipment as its prehistoric ancestors that had evolved to survive tribal environments using Paleolithic instruments. Then consider the techniques and technologies of propaganda. Armed with artificial intelligence, computer modeling, demographic analysis, multinational media industries, millions of dollars, and the latest social psychological insights, propagandists seemed prepared to play the individual like a key on the piano. Modern individuals like to believe that they are at least in control of that tiny slice of their world they call their homes. But even that sense of control is an illusion. Almost every object, purchase, choice, event, relationship, and explanation they consider has been partly processed and delivered by some form of propaganda designed to stimulate just the right reflex. This might be endurable if propaganda always had some kind of paternalistic interest in view. But propagandists tend toward short-term gain power over long-term investment and cooperation. With every looming problem, the most popular propagandas promise the quickest and easiest solutions, even if they mean long-term ruin. Certainly, idealistic-sounding propagandas might claim to aspire to the greater good. But propaganda being focused on the peripheral route seems ready

DOI: 10.4324/9781003607236-7

to always short-circuit central reflection. So when hard choices must be made, propaganda will always fail to make them. Then one day, when catastrophe looms, propaganda will find it more persuasive to send the masses barreling over a cliff rather than sacrifice for collective survival. Proudly, impulsively, eagerly, and *en masse*, human beings will hurl themselves into the abyss with a smile carefully sold to them by propagandists.

But there is also cause not to give way to cynicism and despair. Although certainly this grim view of the future captures many of the enduring problems of propaganda in a mass society, it falls for the slippery slope fallacy so common to apocalyptic projections. If human beings truly acted this way, human civilization would have ended long ago. The image is flawed because it is based on the individual in isolation and without capacity for learning, adaptation, habit, cooperation, sympathy, and growth. If one takes only the Cabbage Patch Riots as one's paradigmatic case, human beings are little more than unruly, spoiled brats. But most people do not act this way in their everyday lives. Even in the year of the "riots" themselves, most of the incidents were few and far between, and the vast majority of shoppers behaved normally. When we look at society at large, we find more continuity and habit than we do frenzy and change. Most people in their work and family lives are creatures of routine, and propaganda messages are largely weak influences that only play a role in the minority of judgments. Even when propaganda worked to radically remake social patterns, as with the COVID-19 pandemic which initiated global lockdowns which were unprecedented growth, it was not enough to make a major dent in our long-term habits. When the pandemic waned, most everyone went back to their familiar patterns of life.

From this perspective, propaganda may actually be seen to be the tool that might save, rather than destroy, human civilization. Human societies are, by their habitual nature, conservative orders. Although propaganda is constantly seeking to stimulate people to accept the new, usually the new gets old, becomes a mere fad, and then fades into the background. The patterns of everyday life return to comfortable streams and canalize action into relatively unremarkable traditions. From this perspective, the greatest danger to human survival is not frenetic distraction and impulsive emotions but rather ordinary blindness, stubbornness, skepticism, and routine.

The challenge of climate change remains quite accurately a problem of consumption, with developed economies like the United States consuming the most resources and releasing the most carbon into the sphere of any country on earth to maintain a high standard of living. What happens, therefore, when global survival depends on collective agreement to limit carbon emissions and reduce energy consumption? The only way to make a mass population agree to such changes is through propaganda, even if it means embracing the "carbon footprint" of BP. It may very well be that survival depends precisely on mobilizing people to mass action and disrupting old habits, which means that our fate depends on propaganda success.

There is also a third position, which is to dismiss this question as ultimately futile and get to work creating propaganda, which is what everyone will do anyway. There simply exists no other practical alternative than to in some way contribute to propaganda if one genuinely wishes to change society at large and adapt to global problems. To simply dismiss propaganda as a pack of lies, to reject it as some kind of offense to human thinking and autonomy, is quite simply to make oneself the subject of other people's propaganda. No one lives on an island. Anyone who communicates at all to anyone else will feel the effects of propaganda, even if only second hand. Propaganda at large is nothing more than the sum total of all competing propagandas happening at any one time, many of them in contention and fighting for different ends. Modern society exists within the cacophony, and it cannot extract itself from it. At the same time that we must be on guard against the glut of disinformation and deception that constantly seems to exploit human weaknesses, we must also commit ourselves to producing better messages.

The point I am trying to make is that propaganda is nothing exotic. It is simply a way of harnessing the means of persuasion by directing them through technique and magnifying them by technology. Whatever the material changes in the way we communicate, at the core of persuasion is the same human desires, thoughts, feelings, fears, anger, ideals, and values that have motivated collective human actions since the invention of language. Undoubtedly, propaganda today exploits all the latest media technologies, artificial intelligences, social science methods of demographic analysis, and algorithmic tools for microtargeting messages. But to pretend that propaganda is something inhuman is to mistake the means for the essence. Propaganda may be cruel, stupid, and irresponsible at times, but that is only because people are capable of acting this way. Propaganda can also be inspired, idealistic, righteous, and committed. It is true that propaganda must always start with the peripheral route to gain interest in a message, but that, too, does not mean that it is wrong. Sometimes impulses and reflexes are precisely what we need to survive. The question is not whether propaganda stimulates reflexes but which one it activates and for what reason.

Propaganda remains one of the most influential arts of modern mass democracy. It is by no means the only one. But for global citizens, propaganda is the medium by which we transcend our national boundaries and address a potentially global public. All members of the new generations understand this fact. It is time that propaganda theory and criticism catch up with what every teenager with a smartphone and social media account already knows—that, for better or for worse, propaganda is a transformative art. We need to accept responsibility for creating and consuming the propaganda that will transform the future into one that we feel worth living. Only through a dedication to an art that continually raises the bar for persuasion, that finds innovative ways to highlight the issues that matter, that provokes passions, thought, and self-respect to energize ordinary people to act together will we have an opportunity to meet the challenges of our time. The future is not one free of propaganda. It is a future in which we have all mastered the techniques of propaganda so that they no longer have the power to master us.

GLOSSARY

Ability   A reference not only to the personal skills, knowledge, and resources a person possesses, but also the time, circumstances, and opportunity to fully consider one's options.

Affect   The dominant quality of an event or object that strikes the viewer during its relatively immediate encounter and provokes some form of impulsive reaction

Agitation propaganda   A category of propaganda that seeks to arouse hatred, contempt, resentment, and indignation against authority by showing it to be fundamentally abusive and unjust.

Anchoring   The notion that people tend to prioritize certain facts, judgments, experiences, and rules that spring to mind first because they are familiar, proximate, or prior.

Analogy   An argument that draws a comparison with a more familiar object and then judges the subject matter of our concern by that standard.

Anger   An emotion characterized by antagonism toward someone or something that you perceive has deliberately done you or someone you care about harm.

Anti-propaganda propaganda   Messaging that deflects from its own propagandistic character by describing propaganda in the most derogatory terms in order to attack others and to flatter one's audience.

Arousal   The degree that affects are felt to be weak or powerful as an experience.

Authentic personality   To possess a unique and striking character that feels to be an expression of a real and permanent substance that is neither superficial nor ephemeral.

Authority The possession of credibility with an audience to the strong degree that one's assertions and conclusions are accepted with relatively unquestioned loyalty and trust.

Bolstering A method of resolving cognitive dissonance that accepts the contradiction but appeals to the conventions of one's surroundings and especially one's favorite peer group.

Brand personality When a brand of consumer products is personified with character traits.

Card stacking The deliberate ordering of facts so that the first piece of data becomes the standard by which subsequent information is judged.

Central route The use of complex reasoning and careful investigation to compare and contrast alternatives before arriving as a decision.

Change A method of resolving cognitive dissonance that chooses one idea and rejects the other.

Cliché A condensed, catchy phrase that defines the meaning of a range of experiences, establishes the nature of the problem, and indicates in the most general way a preferred solution area.

Cognitive dissonance A feeling of discomfort that results from holding two contradictory ideas in one's mind that have a bearing on one's own self-image.

Communication The symbolic sharing of meanings.

Compensatory substitute A tactic of promoting a product, policy, or practice by arousing a basic desire which we were ashamed to admit that we possessed and then providing a socially acceptable vehicle by which that desire is satisfied.

Compliance When we encourage people to perform follow-up behaviors based on a feeling of obligation to meet the social expectations of others.

Covert propaganda When messages are disseminated anonymously or are attributed to a different, usually more recognizable, sender.

Decoy An alternative tactically created to provide a point of comparison and contrast to make another, similar option appear superior.

Deflection source model When a propagandist gives information to a public source who then disseminates it without attribution, as when a negative political campaign feeds a smear to the press but denies doing so.

Denial   A method of resolving cognitive dissonance that denies that cognitive dissonance exists by simply blocking out any messages that would emphasize that dissonance.

Desire   The active impulse to possess or experience something we perceive to be lacking.

Differentiation   A method of resolving cognitive dissonance that freely admits the contradiction exists but uses a difference in situational context to explain and justify its existence.

Disinformation   The deliberate spreading of falsehoods with the intention to deceive.

Distortion   A method of resolving cognitive dissonance that involves changing the premises in such a way that involves misleading manipulation of facts.

Division   A tactic that exploits the natural human impulse to side with one's identified group against the competitor, antagonist, or simply any group not one's own.

Door in the face   When someone makes an initial high demand that is intended to be rejected, followed by a vastly diminished demand that was intended all along.

Dramatic   A characteristic of news stories in which a newsworthy event must contain some element of drama that makes for an engaging story.

Emotion   A dramatized feeling accompanied by pain and pleasure that orients individuals to objects, actions, events, and people within situations marked by change and that contain an implicit judgment.

Environment   The immediate context of actions and the source of our instincts.

Episodic   When new stories feature events as self-contained stories that are largely disconnected from a larger, more complex narrative explanation.

Euphemism   A phrase meant to inspire but to diminish, to make something mundane so that we can turn our attention to other things.

Event   A sequence of happenings and changes in continuous time that can be characterized as having a single, dominant quality.

Eventful   A characteristic of news stories in which it must be an outstanding event that "breaks" into our conscious awareness.

Factoid   An unproven and often unverifiable piece of information, usually in the form of rumors and innuendos, popularized because of the addiction of certain elements of the press for scandal and controversy and shock.

Fake news   Those news stories that are pure inventions created largely to profit from circulation numbers paid advertising.

Fear   The unpleasant emotion caused by the anticipation of harm that will bring pain and suffering to oneself and the people one cares about.

Fiction   A representation of something that is a symbolic creation that cannot, and can never be, equivalent to what it represents.

Foot in the door   When people ask for a very small initial commitment to some idea only to follow up, after a delay, with a more demanding request.

Framing   The dramatic story in which these facts are presented.

Generosity   The voluntary giving of time, resources, and attention to others.

Glittering generalities   Broad value terms that lack any specific denotation yet create a positive or a defining and inspiring but vague ideal.

Granfalloon   A broad, shallow, and easily marked grouping of relative strangers that satisfies the social labels of hierarchy and belonging.

Group mind   Our conception of what other people feel and think that guides our decision-making practices for more than instrumental reasons.

Guilt   The painful feeling of wrongdoing in which people feel to have judged their actions to be some violation of a deeply held value.

Heuristic   A pragmatic cue for solving an immediate, practical problem.

High-spotting   When some event and story dramatizes a single, outstanding quality of something that becomes representative of the entire object or enterprise.

Horizontal propaganda   A category of propaganda that is dialogical and nonhierarchical, relying on conversation and turn-taking, question and answer, community and engagement.

Idea   Any condition of any kind that can be captured in a phrase.

Identification   The symbolic process by which two or more individuals become consubstantial and thereby unified as a group.

Identity   The set of qualities, beliefs, actions, substances, and appearances that characterize a person or a group.

Inference   The process by which the mind makes a leap from the known to the unknown.

Institutional authority   Individuals or groups with titles who function within an established hierarchy and are charged with making and enforcing decisions.

Integration propaganda   A category of propaganda that seeks to reconcile the audience with authority by finding a place for the individual within the social structure.

Interlocking group formations   Interconnected networks of social, economic, and political organizations that develop relationships of cooperation and dependency and which also allow individuals to participate in multiple spheres of practice simultaneously.

Irrational propaganda   A category of propaganda that relies on caricature and basic appeals to binary emotions.

Judgment   A determination by oneself that this violation was not justified or excusable.

Known   That which we perceive before us and what we take for granted.

Legitimating source model   When a propagandist gives anonymous information to a public source, but then the propagandist actively cites that source as proof of the legitimacy of their message.

Lowballing   When one makes a low demand of expenditure of money, resources, or time for some commodity or venture knowing that it will be accepted, only to add more demands to the initial price after a delay.

Mass individuals   People whose lives and livelihoods are dependent on the institutions and resources of a postindustrial technological society.

Modification   A method of resolving cognitive dissonance that entails altering the premises and facts of one or both sides in order to show that there is no actual contradiction.

Mood   A pervasive feeling experienced by a person that seems not related at all to external objects, but rather originates within the self and pervades an atmosphere.

Motivation A desire to exert energy and overcome resistance to produce an outcome that is deemed important for the person's well-being.

Motive A compelling and self-conscious reason for acting.

Myth A sweeping narrative of origins and destinies that provides enduring models of action and value that are recurrent over time and which potentially answer all questions in vague but emotionally satisfying ways.

News Information about what is new that grows out of a very basic human desire to know what is going on.

News media An industry that produces, dramatizes, and disseminates new information that is designed to capture the attention of the buying public.

Norm of commitment We have an obligation to follow through on our promises.

Norm of reciprocity We should pay someone back for what we perceive to be an act of generosity.

Objective To construct a report that references tangible objects, events, people, records, statements, and actions that are open to others to experience independently on their own.

Opinion leaders Those who are simply persuasive authorities for particular social groups, who then disseminate and translate these messages to their followers.

Overhearing A tactic that conveys what appears to be one's "real opinion" through a private communication that is made to seem inadvertently broadcast to the public.

Over-simplification When misleading or even false qualities are made central to the representation in order to manipulate an audience into believing what is clearly untrue or even harmful.

Overt propaganda A message that accurately identifies the author and is explicit about the aims and intentions of the propagandist

Packaging An accessible outward presentation of something crafted specifically to be easily recognized and interpreted by a mass audience as satisfying or threatening some interest.

Passions A particular set of emotions that tend to be the most instinctive and volatile.

Peripheral route Mental processing that takes the quickest shortcut based on simple cues.

Personal A characteristic of news stories that features the actions of key players as antagonists or protagonists, even if there are many other people involved and many other factors at play.

Persuasion The use of symbols to change attitudes and beliefs.

Persuasive authority The use of symbolic appeals to values, aims, and knowledge to convince people to voluntarily adopt certain practices and adhere to particular rules.

Political propaganda A category of propaganda that is produced by a distinct group with clear identity and interests who advocate for distinct ideas, actions, and policies.

Power The ability to act with confidence in a practical or social setting.

Propaganda A set of modern techniques for producing, organizing, and directing the reflexes of a mass of individuals by creating events, crafting identity, simplifying ideas, and arousing passions.

Pseudo-environment A picture of the world outside of our direct experience that is created through symbols and yet guides action that has impacts on actual reality.

Media event An active happening that is intentionally designed to draw attention from the news media to be broadcast to the public.

Quality The dominant quality that a thing possesses in a particular encounter.

Question asking Using a dialogic question and answer format to more directly implicate the audience in the process of judgment.

Rational propaganda A category of propaganda that represents this effort to drown its audience and facts in order to build out of this chaos a vague but powerful mythic conclusion.

Rationalization The process of reflecting on past actions and coming up with an account that justifies or at least explains them.

Rationalization trap A tactic that deliberately arouses cognitive dissonance and then provides a rationalization for resolving that dissonance that serves the interests of the propagandist.

Reason A capacity to use logic and investigate a problem and arrive at a solution or explanation.

Reflex   A patterned response to recognizable stimuli that satisfy some immediate input.

Rhetoric   The art of persuasion that seeks to direct action and constitute judgment within a situation marked by uncertainty and urgency.

Scarcity   The quality of not being readily available without considerable effort to attain it, as in the social heuristic that tells us that what is scarce, or hard to attain, is also that which is desirable for others.

Self-sacrifice   When a person gives up something one genuinely treasures for the sake of benefiting a cause and helping others.

Sign   An index in the material world that directly indicates the presence of something else.

Simplifying ideas   The process of making complicated, abstract, or distant matters easy to understand, concrete, and relevant to an audience in a way that stimulates peripheral route processing and provokes reflex actions desired by the propagandist.

Sociological propaganda   A category of propaganda that is a diffuse, long-term effort to alter general attitudes and norms through the medium of cultural and social institutions, leisure activities, consumption practices, and habits.

Spokesperson   When an individual speaks in support of or on behalf of another individual or group for the purposes of bolstering their reputation and credibility.

Symbol   That which has only an arbitrary connection with its object dictated by convention and use.

Techniques   Efficient methods that have largely been stripped of their cultural specificity or personal flair and have been turned into mathematical formulas that guarantee universal outcome.

Technological society   A society marked by the development of industrial, transportation, and communication technologies, the rise in the authority of science and scientific method, the appearance of high-density urban populations, the breakdown of the isolated local community, the increase in mobility and specialization, and the expansion of the power of corporations and the state.

That's not all   A technique that uses reciprocity as a sales tactic whereby a product or idea is sold at a certain cost or price, before judgment is made, added benefits or qualities are added on for "free."

Timely A characteristic of news stories that insists that the events must not only be new but also relevant in some way to the contemporary situation.

Transcendence A method of resolving cognitive dissonance that adopts a position above an apparent contradiction so that it no longer appears to be a contradiction anymore from a perspective of height.

Truth A fictional representations that provides reliable pictures of the world on which people can act.

Unknown That which isn't immediately present to our awareness.

Valence The positive or negative orientation of that quality as it is received by the viewer.

Value Any image of an ideal action or event that might be captured in a principle, law, or definition that is actively sought after and treasured by an individual.

Vertical propaganda A category of propaganda that is top-down propaganda delivered by a single source, usually through a mass medium, to be consumed simultaneously by a large audience.

Violation A specific act that has either contradicted or at least not lived up to the standard of the value.

Vivid appeal A highly detailed, specific, dramatic, and memorable example of some event to stand in for an entire range of experiences in order to provoke an immediate reaction based on that example alone.

REFERENCES

"Are you better off than you were 4 years ago?" WBUR, September 11, 2012, https://www.wbur.org/cognoscenti/2012/09/11/better-off-2012-elaine-kamarck

"Are you a Pepper?" Dr. Pepper Museum, https://drpeppermuseum.com/are-you-a-pepper/

Arendt, Hannah. *The Origins of Totalitarianism*. New York: Harcourt, 1976.

Barr, Jason M. "Clouds in your coffee? Skyscrapers and their symbolic heights," Building the Skyline, January 20, 2021, https://buildingtheskyline.org/skyscrapers-and-symbolic-height/

Bastidas, Igor. "Worrying about your carbon footprint is exactly what big oil wants you to do," *The Guardian*, August 31, 2021, https://www.theguardian.com/environment/2019/aug/28/greta-thunberg-arrival-in-new-york-delayed-by-rough-seas

Behrmann, Anna. "The artists of Extinction Rebellion: 'Our bold imagery is helping to change the conversations around climate change'," *i*, November 24, 2019, https://inews.co.uk/culture/arts/extinction-rebellion-artist-protest-banner-art-red-rebel-flag-logo-366404?srsltid=AfmBOoopEuNci5pBaUQwt33LewsJCwFUQaei_ZDxW8l5JA7un7yFZH66

Belluz, Julia. "Fighting scary vaccine stories with scarier no-vaccine stories," Macleans, June 7, 2012, https://macleans.ca/society/health/fighting-scary-vaccine-stories-with-scarier-ones/

Bennett, W. Lance. *News: The Politics of Illusion*, 10th Edition. Chicago: University of Chicago Press, 2016.

Bernays, Edward. *Propaganda*. New York: Ig Publishing, 2004.

Black, Rebecca "Twelfth of July festivities 'about celebration' – DUP leader," *Independent*, July 11, 2024, https://www.the-independent.com/news/uk/gavin-robinson-northern-ireland-dup-ireland-irish-b2578144.html

"BP Ad: Carbon Footprint," https://www.youtube.com/watch?v=ywr ZPypqSB4

Bubbosh, Paul. "Rethinking 'Think Globally, Act Locally'," George Mason University, https://cesp.gmu.edu/rethinking-think-globally-act-locally/

Buddy, T. "Going to your first 12-step meeting," Very Well Mind, October 12, 2023, https://www.verywellmind.com/what-can-i-expect-at-a-12-step-meeting-63409

Burke, Kenneth. *On Symbols and Society*, edited by Joseph Gusfield. Chicago: University of Chicago Press, 1989.

Burke, Kenneth. *The War of Words*, edited by Anthony Burke, Kyle Jensen, and Jack Selzer. Oakland, CA: University of California Press, 2018.

Buttelman, Michel. "Everyone's Irish on St. Patrick's Day," The Signal, March 13, 2022 https://signalscv.com/2022/03/everyones-irish-on-st-patricks-day/

Cadwalladr, Carole. "'I made Steve Bannon's psychological warfare tool': Meet the data war whistleblower," *The Guardian*, March 18, 2018, https://www.theguardian.com/news/2018/mar/17/data-war-whistleblower-christopher-wylie-faceook-nix-bannon-trump

Calista, C. "What the happiest place on earth can teach us about happiness," Medium, August 24, 2022, https://medium.com/illumination/what-the-happiest-place-on-earth-can-teach-us-about-happiness-706ea6c9e9e2

Carroll, Rory. "'Government is not listening': anger over immigration spills into riot on Dublin's streets," *The Guardian*, November 24, 2023, https://www.theguardian.com/world/2023/nov/24/anger-immigration-riot-dublin-ireland

Casserly, Meghan. "Grilling, guys and the great gender divide," *Forbes*, July 19, 2013, https://www.forbes.com/2010/07/01/grilling-men-women-barbecue-forbes-woman-time-cooking.html

Castells, Manuel. *Networks of Outrage and Hope: Social Movements in the Internet Age*. Cambridge, UK: Polity Press, 2012.

Castillo, Mariano. "Venezuela: Will 'Chavismo' survive?" CNN, March 11, 2013, https://www.cnn.com/2013/03/09/world/americas/venezuela-chavismo/index.html

"Chili's is launching a new campaign created by Mischief called 'you deserve them more than kids do'," Ads of Brands, September 18, 2023, https://adsofbrands.net/en/news/chili%E2%80%99s-is-launching-a-new-campaign-created-by-mischief-called-you-deserve-them-more-than-kids-do/5042

Cohen, Jamie. "How KONY 2012 trained the audience — and YouTube — to love reactionary media," Medium, March 4, 2002, https://onezero.medium.com/how-kony-2012-trained-the-audience-and-youtube-to-love-reactionary-media-f3c38435ba58

"Community Assemblies Escalation Plan," Extinction Rebellion, https://extinctionrebellion.uk/act-now/campaigns/community-assemblies-escalation-plan/

Corrigan, Maureen. "The incredible story of Chilean miners rescued from the 'deep down dark'," NPR, October 29, 2014, https://www.npr.org/2014/10/29/359839104/the-incredible-story-of-chilean-miners-rescued-from-the-deep-down-dark

"Covid-19 fueling Anti-Asian racism and xenophobia worldwide," Human Rights Watch, May 12, 2020, https://www.hrw.org/news/2020/05/12/covid-19-fueling-anti-asian-racism-and-xenophobia-worldwide

Crick, Nathan. *Rhetorical Public Speaking: Social Influence in the Digital Age*, 4th Edition. New York: Routledge, 2023.

Criss, Doug "This is the 30-year-old Willie Horton ad everybody is talking about today," CNN, November 1, 2018, https://www.cnn.com/2018/11/01/politics/willie-horton-ad-1988-explainer-trnd/index.html

Dahlberg, Brett and Elena Renken, "New Coronavirus disease officially named COVID-19 by the World Health Organization," NPR, February 11, 2020, https://www.npr.org/sections/goatsandsoda/2020/02/11/802352351/new-coronavirus-gets-an-official-name-from-the-world-health-organization

"Dennis Rodman: 'People don't see … the good side' of North Korea," ABC News, June 23, 2017, https://abcnews.go.com/International/dennis-rodman-people-good-side-north-korea/story?id=48224976

Diaz, Danielle. "3 times Trump defended his 'locker room' talk," CNN, October 9, 2016, https://www.cnn.com/2016/10/09/politics/donald-trump-locker-room-talk-presidential-debate-2016-election/index.html

"Does the concept of the Third World have any historical value?" *History Today*, April 4, 2023, https://www.historytoday.com/archive/head-head/does-concept-third-world-have-any-historical-value

"Dr. Pepper - 'Be a Pepper' with David Naughton (Commercial, 1978)," https://www.youtube.com/watch?v=YXQzaD168FA

"Dutch football hooligans wreak havoc in Rome," Wanted in Rome, February 19, 2015, https://www.wantedinrome.com/news/dutch-football-hooligans-wreak-havoc-in-rome.html

Eastwood, Brian. "Sam Altman believes AI will change the world (and everything else)," MIT Sloan School of Management, May 8, 2024, https://mitsloan.mit.edu/ideas-made-to-matter/sam-altman-believes-ai-will-change-world-and-everything-else

Elliott, Philip. "Why some suspect Christie's hot mic moment was no accident," *Time*, January 11, 2024, https://time.com/6554200/chris-christie-hot-mic-comments/

Ellul, Jacques. *Propaganda: The Formation of Men's Attitudes*. New York: Vintage, 1965.

Elsesser, Kim. "Here's how Instagram harms young women according to research," *Forbes*, October 10, 2021, https://www.forbes.com/sites/kimelsesser/2021/10/05/heres-how-instagram-harms-young-women-according-to-research/

"Etymology of 'Factoid'," *Irregardless Magazine*, August 17, 2019, https://www.irregardlessmagazine.com/articles/etymology-of-factoid/

Eveleth, Rose. "The biggest lie tech people tell themselves—and the rest of us," Vox, October 8, 2019, https://www.vox.com/the-highlight/2019/10/1/20887003/tech-technology-evolution-natural-inevitable-ethics

"Fighting Hate," SPLC, https://www.splcenter.org/fighting-hate

Forbes, Ellie. "Scotch Whisky distilleries attract more than 2 million visitors," Scottish Field, September 27, 2023, https://www.scottishfield.co.uk/food-and-drink-2/scotch-whisky-distilleries-attract-more-than-2-million-visitors/

Fredell, Benjamin. "My affair with Spotify's AI DJ," *The Tacoma Ledger*, February 19, 2024.

"Grace: peta2's Thanksgiving ad," PETA, https://www.peta.org/videos/grace-peta2s-thanksgiving-ad/

Griffin, Jonathan. "Incels: Inside a dark world of online hate," BBC News, August 13, 2021, https://www.bbc.com/news/blogs-trending-44053828

Gunders, Dana. "Super size, super waste: What whopping portions do to the planet," Grist, October 15, 2012, https://grist.org/food/super-size-super-waste/

Hanscomb, Stuart. *Critical Thinking: The Basics*, 2nd Edition. New York: Routledge, 2023.

Hern, Alex. "Cambridge Analytica: How did it turn clicks into votes?" *The Guardian*, May 6, 2018, https://www.theguardian.com/news/2018/may/06/cambridge-analytica-how-turn-clicks-into-votes-christopher-wylie

Hoffman, Christopher. "Cabbage Patch Kids Riots: 40-year anniversary of toy-induced pandemonium," WPDE News, November 24, 2023, https://wpde.com/news/nation-world/reliving-the-cabbage-patch-doll-craze-of-1983-zayre-walmart-dolls-mob-coleco-christmas-new-york

Horwitz, Sari, Scott Higham, Dalton Bennett and Meryl Kornfield, "The Opioid Files: Inside the opioid industry's marketing machine," *The Washington Post*, December 6, 2019, https://www.washingtonpost.com/graphics/2019/investigations/opioid-marketing/

"How filter bubbles distort reality: Everything you need to know," Farnam Street, https://fs.blog/filter-bubbles/

"Hungary: Propaganda Law has "created cloud of fear" pushing LGBTI+ community into the shadows," Amnesty International, February 27, 2024, https://www.amnesty.org/en/latest/news/2024/02/hungarypropaganda-law-has-created-cloud-of-fear-pushing-lgbti-community-into-the-shadows/

Hyken, Shep. "Selling to Gen-Z: This is what they want," *Forbes*, June 30, 2022, https://www.forbes.com/sites/shephyken/2022/06/12/selling-to-gen-z-this-is-what-they-want/

"'I can't breathe': The refrain that reignited a movement," Amnesty International, June 30, 2020, https://www.amnesty.org/en/latest/news/2020/06/i--cant-breathe-refrain-reignited-movement/#:~:text=Three%20words%20uttered%20by%20George,U.S.%20and%20across%20the%20globe

"In speech at the UN, Bolsonaro plays down environmental crisis and disregards secularism," Conectas, https://www.conectas.org/en/noticias/in-speech-at-the-un-bolsonaro-plays-down-environmental-crisis-and-disregards-secularism/

"India – Tobacco Control – When You Quit," Vital Strategies, https://www.vitalstrategies.org/resources/india-tobacco-control-when-you-quit/#:~:text=The%20campaign%20video%20has%20been,tobacco%2Dfree%20film%20rules%20legislation

"Introducing Brewer Patriot Ale," Sam Adams Boston Taproom, https://www.samadamsbostontaproom.com/blog/2021/introducing-brewer-patriot-ale

Jankowicz, Mia. "The coronavirus outbreak has prompted people around the world to panic buy toilet paper. Here's why," *Business Insider*, March 10, 2020, https://www.businessinsider.com/coronavirus-panic-buying-toilet-paper-stockpiling-photos-2020-3

Jasper, James M. *The Art of Moral Protest: Culture, Biography, and Creativity in Social Movements*. Chicago: University of Chicago Press, 1997

Jefferson, Thomas. "From Thomas Jefferson to Samuel Adams, 29 March 1801," Founders Online, https://founders.archives.gov/documents/Jefferson/01-33-02-0421

"Jimmy and Rosalynn Carter," Habitat for Humanity, https://www.habitat.org/ap/about/how-we-began/role-of-jimmy-and-rosalynn-carter

Jowett, Garth S. and Victoria O'Donnell. *Readings in Propaganda and Persuasion: New and Classic Essays*. Thousand Oaks, CA: Sage, 2005.

Kahney, Leander. "Apple: It's all about the brand," Wired, December 4, 2002, https://www.wired.com/2002/12/apple-its-all-about-the-brand/

Kennedy, George. *Aristotle, on Rhetoric: A Theory of Civic Discourse*, 2nd Edition. Oxford: Oxford University Press, 2006.

"Khaled Said: The face that launched a revolution," Abram Online, June 6, 2012, https://english.ahram.org.eg/NewsContent/1/0/43995/Egypt/0/Khaled-Said-The-face-that-launched-a-revolution.aspx

Knightley, Phillip "The disinformation campaign," *The Guardian*, October 4, 2001, https://www.theguardian.com/education/2001/oct/04/socialsciences.highereducation

Kolesnikov, Andrei. "How Putin's "special military operation" became a people's war," Carnegie Politika, April 10, 2023, https://

carnegieendowment.org/russia-eurasia/politika/2023/03/how-putins-special-military-operation-became-a-peoples-war?lang=en

Kulish, Nicholas and Kelly K. SporsStaff, "Bracing for a terror attack: First, pick up the duct tape," *The Wall Street Journal*, February 11, 2003, https://www.wsj.com/articles/SB1044820213906360703

Lakoff, George and Mark Johnson, *Metaphors We Live By*. Chicago: University of Chicago Press, 1980.

Leber, Rebecca. "Why Americans will pay higher natural gas prices this winter," Vox, November 24, 2022, https://www.vox.com/policy-and-politics/23462844/natural-gas-us-prices-winter-2022

Lewis, Neil A. "Ex-Cheney aide testified leak was ordered, prosecutor says," *The New York Times*, February 10, 2006, https://www.nytimes.com/2006/02/10/politics/excheney-aide-testified-leak-was-ordered-prosecutor-says.html

"Libya migrant 'slave market' footage sparks outrage," BBC News, November 18, 2017, https://www.bbc.com/news/world-africa-42038451

Lippmann, Walter. *Public Opinion*. New York: The Free Press, 1997.

Lockwood, Robert P. "Giordano Bruno: How fact becomes anti-Catholic fiction," Catholic Answers, November 1, 2009, https://www.catholic.com/magazine/print-edition/how-fact-becomes-anti-catholic-fiction

Loewentheil, Hannah. "24 subtle signs that often signal that a restaurant is, in fact, VERY good," BuzzFeed, June 5, 2023, https://www.buzzfeed.com/hannahloewentheil/people-are-sharing-green-flags-in-restaurants-that-signal

Longfellow, Henry Wadsworth. "Paul Revere's Ride," Paul Revere House, https://www.paulreverehouse.org/longfellows-poem/

Lorenz, Taylor. "To fight vaccine lies, authorities recruit an 'influencer army'," *The New York Times*, August 1, 2021, https://www.nytimes.com/2021/08/01/technology/vaccine-lies-influencer-army.html

Lowe, Josh. "Brexit: UKIP launches 'Breaking Point' immigration poster," *Newsweek*, June 16, 2016, https://www.newsweek.com/brexit-eu-immigration-ukip-poster-breaking-point-471081

Lynas, Mark. "COVID: Top 10 current conspiracy theories," Alliance for Science, https://allianceforscience.org/blog/2020/04/covid-top-10-current-conspiracy-theories/

MacFarlane, Drew "Trump uses winter storm to mock climate change, confuses weather and climate again," The Weather Channel, January 21, 2019, https://weather.com/science/environment/news/2019-01-21-trump-alludes-to-winter-storm-to-mock-climate-change

Madden, Emma. "'Kony 2012,' 10 years later," *The New York Times*, March 8, 2022, https://www.nytimes.com/2022/03/08/style/kony-2012-invisible-children.html

Margolin, Emma. "'Make America great again'—who said it first?," NBC News, September 9, 2016, https://www.nbcnews.com/politics/2016-election/make-america-great-again-who-said-it-first-n645716

Marsh, Viv. "China to overhaul 'threatening' one-child slogans," BBC News, February 27, 2012, https://www.bbc.com/news/world-asia-17181951

McBride, James. "How Green-Party success is reshaping global politics," Council on Foreign Relations, May 5, 2022, https://www.cfr.org/backgrounder/how-green-party-success-reshaping-global-politics

Merrill, Jeremy B. and Will Oremus, "Five points for anger, one for a 'like': How Facebook's formula fostered rage and misinformation," *The Washington Post*, October 26, 2021, https://www.washingtonpost.com/technology/2021/10/26/facebook-angry-emoji-algorithm/

Miller, Zoë. "11 famous movie and TV locations that locals say have been ruined by tourists," *Business Insider*, November 3, 2022, https://www.businessinsider.com/famous-movie-and-tv-locations-ruined-by-tourism-2020-2

Morton, Victor. "Greta Thunberg carbon-reduced plan blown by flight of captain," *Washington Times*, December 1, 2019,https://www.washingtontimes.com/news/2019/dec/1/greta-thunberg-carbon-reduced-plan-blown-flight-ca/

Mostegel, Iris. "Edward Bernays: The original influencer," *History Today*, February 6, 2019, https://www.historytoday.com/miscellanies/original-influencer

Nakashima, Ellen and Shane Harris, "How the Russians hacked the DNC and passed its emails to WikiLeaks," *The Washington Post*, July 13, 2018, https://www.washingtonpost.com/world/national-security/how-the-russians-hacked-the-dnc-and-passed-its-emails-to-wikileaks/2018/07/13/af19a828-86c3-11e8-8553-a3ce89036c78_story.html

Ni, Perla. "Why vivid storytelling inspires giving," *Stanford Social Innovation Review*, February 5, 2008, https://ssir.org/articles/entry/why_vivid_storytelling_inspires_giving

Niranjan, Ajit. "Anger is most powerful emotion by far for spurring climate action, study finds," *The Guardian*, August 21, 2023, https://www.theguardian.com/environment/2023/aug/21/anger-is-most-powerful-emotion-by-far-for-spurring-climate-action-study-finds

Nix, Jessica. "Swifties set off 2.3 quake in Seattle," *Forbes*, July 28, 2023, https://www.forbes.com/sites/jessicanix/2023/07/28/swifties-set-off-23-quake-in-seattle/

"Nude calendar stunt helps pave Sask. highway," CBC News, November 5, 2010, https://www.cbc.ca/news/canada/saskatchewan/nude-calendar-stunt-helps-pave-sask-highway-1.963358

Oddo, John. *The Discourse of Propaganda: Case Studies from the Persian Gulf War and the War on Terror*. University Park, PA: The Pennsylvania State University Press, 2018.

Olejnik, Lukasz. *Propaganda: From Disinformation and Influence to Operations and Information Warfare*. New York: Routledge, 2024.

Orwell, George. *All Art Is Propaganda: Critical Essays*, edited by George Packer. New York: Houghton Mifflin, 2008.

"Paris Mayor Anne Hidalgo swims in the Seine nine days before Olympic Games kickoff," France24, July 17, 2024, https://www.france24.com/en/france/20240717-paris-mayor-anne-hidalgo-swims-in-the-seine-nine-days-before-olympic-games-kickoff

"Paul Revere's engraving of the Boston Massacre, 1770," The Gilder Lehrman Institute of American History, https://www.gilderlehrman.org/history-resources/spotlight-primary-source/paul-reveres-engraving-boston-massacre-1770

Peters, Mark. "George Carlin: Euphemism fighter supreme," McSweeney's, May 19, 2017, https://www.mcsweeneys.net/articles/george-carlin-euphemism-fighter-supreme

Pierce, Yolanda. "Righteous anger, Black Lives Matter, and the legacy of King," Berkeley Center for Religion, Peace, and World Affairs, January 16, 2018, https://berkleycenter.georgetown.edu/responses/righteous-anger-black-lives-matter-and-the-legacy-of-king

Pratkanis, Anthony and Elliot Aronson. *Age of Propaganda: The Everyday Use and Abuse of Persuasion*. New York: Henry Holt, 2001.

"Press Briefing by Press Secretary Jen Psaki, August 10, 2021," The White House, https://www.whitehouse.gov/briefing-room/press-briefings/2021/08/10/press-briefing-by-press-secretary-jen-psaki-august-10-2021/

Prisco, Jacopo. "Keep calm: The story behind the UK's most famous poster design," CNN, November 1, 2017, https://www.cnn.com/style/article/keep-calm-poster/index.html

"Proclamation: Black Lives Matter Day," Black Lives Matter, July 10, 2023, https://blacklivesmatter.com/blm-day/

"Propaganda at the movies," Facing History and Ourselves, August 2, 2016, https://www.facinghistory.org/resource-library/propaganda-movies

"QAnon," ADL, October 28, 2022, https://www.adl.org/resources/backgrounder/qanon

"Quick Guide. What is the Running of the Bulls," SanFermin.com, https://www.sanfermin.com/en/running-of-the-bulls/quick-guide-what-is-the-running-of-the-bulls/

Ray, Craig. "SA's flag symbolises success and unity on the sports fields and doesn't deserve 'burning'," Daily Maverick, May 7, 2024, https://www.dailymaverick.co.za/article/2024-05-07-sas-flag-symbolises-success-and-unity-on-the-sports-fields-and-doesnt-deserve-burning/

"Rebuilding the ozone layer: How the world came together for the ultimate repair job," UN Environmental Program, September 15, 2021, https://www.unep.org/news-and-stories/story/rebuilding-ozone-layer-how-world-came-together-ultimate-repair-job

Restrepo, Manuela López. "Just Do It: How the iconic Nike tagline built a career for the late Dan Wieden," NPR, October 6, 2022, https://www.npr.org/2022/10/06/1127032721/nike-just-do-it-slogan-success-dan-wieden-kennedy-dies

"Russian militia attacks Pussy Riot members in Sochi," CBS News, February 19, 2014, https://www.cbsnews.com/news/pussy-riot-attacked-at-winter-olympics-2014-by-cossacks-in-sochi/

Said-Moorhouse, Lauren, Florence Obondo, and Marc Hoeferlin, "Olajumoke Adenowo: Nigeria's star architect on how she made it," CNN, January 5, 2015, https://www.cnn.com/2014/12/04/world/africa/olajumoke-adenowo-nigerias-star-architect/index.html

Sandwith, Corinne. "Mayibuye! The 100-year-old slogan that's stirred up divisions in South Africa's elections," The Conversation, May 27, 2024, https://theconversation.com/mayibuye-the-100-year-old-slogan-thats-stirred-up-divisions-in-south-africas-elections-230985

Schendler, Auden, "Worrying about Your Carbon Footprint Is Exactly What Big Oil Wants You to Do," *The New York Times*, August 31, 2021, https://www.nytimes.com/2021/08/31/opinion/climate-change-carbon-neutral.html

Schwartz, Mattathias. "A trail of 'bread crumbs,' leading conspiracy theorists into the wilderness," *The New York Times*, September 11, 2018, https://www.nytimes.com/2018/09/11/magazine/a-trail-of-bread-crumbs-leading-conspiracy-theorists-into-the-wilderness.html

Shapiro, Paul. "Vegan: The product label which shall not be named," FoodDive, Oct. 5, 2023, https://www.fooddive.com/news/vegan-the-product-label-which-shall-not-be-named/695501/

Shaw, Neil. "Why barbecuing is still seen as a man's job," *Wales Online*, May 30, 2023, https://www.walesonline.co.uk/whats-on/food-drink-news/barbecuing-still-seen-mans-job-27019484

Shwartz, A. Brad. "The infamous "War of the Worlds" radio broadcast was a magnificent fluke," *Smithsonian Magazine*, May 6, 2015, https://www.smithsonianmag.com/history/infamous-war-worlds-radio-broadcast-was-magnificent-fluke-180955180/

Siddique, Abubakar and Mansoor Khosrow, "Afghanistan's Shi'ite minority suffers 'systematic discrimination' under Taliban rule," Radio Free Europe Radio Liberty, July 17, 2023, https://www.rferl.org/a/afghanistan-taliban-shiite-persecution-discrimination/32507042.html

"Snail of Approval," Slow Food USA, https://slowfoodusa.org/snail-of-approval/

Snow, Nancy, Garth S. Jowett, and Victoria O'Donnell. *Propaganda & Persuasion*, 8th Edition. Thousand Oaks, CA: Sage, 2024.

Stanley, Jason. *How Fascism Works: The Politics of Us and Them*. New York: Random House, 2018.

Stanley, Jason. *How Propaganda Works*. Princeton, NJ: Princeton University Press, 2015.

Stockman, Farah, Kate Kelly, and Jennifer Medina, "How buying beans became a political statement," *The New York Times*, July 19, 2020, https://www.nytimes.com/2020/07/19/us/goya-trump-hispanic-vote.html

Syed, Armani. "Why protesters are squirting water at tourists in Barcelona," *Time*, July 8, 2024, https://time.com/6995756/barcelona-protesters-water-pistols-tourists/

Taylor, Philip M. *Munitions of the Mind: A History of Propaganda*, 3rd Edition. Manchester, UK: Manchester University Press, 2004.

"The family fallout shelter," Office of Civil and Defense Mobilization, Prelinger Library: San Francisco, 2008. https://www.survivorlibrary.com/library/the_family_fallout_shelter_1959.pdf

"The saga of 'Pizzagate': The fake story that shows how conspiracy theories spread," BBC, December 2, 2016,https://www.bbc.com/news/blogs-trending-38156985

"The sinister shadow of Giordano Bruno in Campo de' Fiori," Through Eternity Tours, February 17, 2021, https://www.througheternity.com/en/blog/hidden-sights/campo_de_fiori_sinister_shadow_bruno.html

Treisman, Rachel. "Putin's claim of fighting against Ukraine 'neo-Nazis' distorts history, scholars say," NPR, March 1, 2022, https://www.npr.org/2022/03/01/1083677765/putin-denazify-ukraine-russia-history

"Ulster Defence Association," Britannica, https://www.britannica.com/topic/Ulster-Defence-Association

van Gelder, Sarah. "'Slow Food' pioneer's love for food ripened into a life's work," United Nations University, June 1, 2016, https://ourworld.unu.edu/en/slow-food-pioneers-love-for-food-ripened-into-a-lifes-work

Waxman, Olivia B. "'He was sent by God to take care of us': Inside the real story behind Schindler's list," *Time*, December 7, 2018, https://time.com/5470613/schindlers-list-true-story/

"We Can Do It!" National Museum of American History, https://americanhistory.si.edu/collections/nmah_538122

Weingarten, Gene. "Pearls before breakfast: Can one of the nation's great musicians cut through the fog of a D.C. rush hour? Let's find out," *The Washington Post*, April 8, 2007, https://www.washingtonpost.com/lifestyle/magazine/pearls-before-breakfast-can-one-of-the-nations-great-musicians-cut-through-the-fog-of-a-dc-rush-hour-lets-find-out/2014/09/23/8a6d46da-4331-11e4-b47c-f5889e061e5f_story.html

Wells, Ione. "Mining giants sign $30bn settlement for 2015 Brazil dam collapse," BBC News, October 25, 2024, https://www.bbc.com/news/articles/cx2dk8yy4kjo

"What is the greenhouse effect?" NASA, https://science.nasa.gov/climate-change/faq/what-is-the-greenhouse-effect/

"'When you ride ALONE you ride with Hitler!' U.S. Government Propaganda Poster, 1943," Energy History, https://energyhistory.yale.edu/when-you-ride-alone-you-ride-with-hitler-u-s-government-propaganda-poster-1943/

Wilcox, Christie. "What does a positive Covid test look like?," The Scientist, May 10, 2024, https://www.the-scientist.com/what-does-a-positive-covid-test-look-like-68965

Will, Madeline. "Misogynist influencer Andrew Tate has captured boys' attention: What teachers need to know," EducationWeek, February 2, 2023, https://www.edweek.org/leadership/misogynist-influencer-andrew-tate-has-captured-boys-attention-what-teachers-need-to-know/2023/02

Wilson, Una. "Maui wildfires shed light on environmental justice issues closer to home," Old Gold & Black, September 7, 2023, https://wfuogb.com/20832/environment/maui-wildfires-shed-light-on-environmental-justice-issues-closer-to-home/

"Wine study shows price influences perception," Caltech, January 14, 2008, https://www.caltech.edu/about/news/wine-study-shows-price-influences-perception-1374

"World media hail Messi, Mbappé after 'most exciting final' in World Cup history," France 24, December 19, 2022, https://www.france24.com/en/sport/20221219-world-media-hail-messi-mbapp%C3%A9-after-most-exciting-final-in-world-cup-history

"Your guide to Fairtrade labeling," Fair Trade America, April 19, 2021, https://www.fairtradeamerica.org/news-insights/your-guide-to-fairtrade-labeling/

INDEX

For Product Safety Concerns and Information please contact our EU
representative GPSR@taylorandfrancis.com
Taylor & Francis Verlag GmbH, Kaufingerstraße 24, 80331 München, Germany